INTO MUSIC

Book 1

PETER BROWN

Senior Music Lecturer
Bedford College of Physical Education

Consultant Editor
James Kirkpatrick

Head of Music
King Edward's School, Witley

Hulton Educational

Acknowledgement
The publishers are very grateful to the British Broadcasting
Corporation for allowing them to reproduce the song 'Flying
Machines' by Douglas Coombes, from *Time and Tune* (1975).

First published in Great Britain 1983
by Hulton Educational Publications Ltd
Raans Road, Amersham, Bucks HP6 6JJ

Text © *Peter Brown* 1983
Illustrations © *Hulton Educational* 1983

Edited and designed by James Shepherd
Artwork by Philip Schramm

ISBN 0 7175 1097 2

Printed in Great Britain by The Pitman Press, Bath

Contents

1 RAW MATERIALS

Vibrations

All sounds are caused by a very fast shaking —or VIBRATION. These vibrations, which you can sometimes feel or see, are much too fast to count. Musical instruments must vibrate:

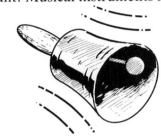

Sometimes the whole instrument vibrates

or just a part of it

The air inside any tube vibrates as well

Feel or see the vibrations in the following activities.

Things to do

1. Sing any song while gently touching the front of your throat.
2. Play the song on comb and paper.
3. Gently touch the edge of a ringing bell or similar object. What happens if you grasp it?
4. Feel or see the vibrations on other instruments.

But it is not only instruments that vibrate. Whenever you hear a sound, there must be a vibration:

In your notebook

(i) (Copy, completing the words)
All sounds are caused by v——. If you touch certain instruments or objects the v—— can even be f——.

Things to do

5. Assemble material such as leaves, blades of grass, drinking straws, balloons and silver paper. Feel the vibrations on your lips or fingers as you try to get sounds out of them.
6. Now experiment with other objects that can make interesting sounds, such as bottles, jars, pen-tops and rulers.
7. Use objects from 5 and 6 in the following. Decide on an order of playing related to seating position and pass a chain of sounds round the room. Play as soon as you hear the player before you. Time the chain and see if the reverse order is quicker. Suggest other ways of playing the chain, for example, each play three sounds, have races between rows or play with eyes closed.
8. Watch as teacher or pupil-players demonstrate their musical instruments. Notice (a) what they do to start and stop the vibrations and (b) how long sounds are played.

Instruments

You are likely to have a number of the following instruments in your classroom. Some others may be brought by pupils. Study the pictures, which group instruments according to playing method. Think about where the vibrations occur, how they are started and stopped and whether they are 'caught' by other parts:

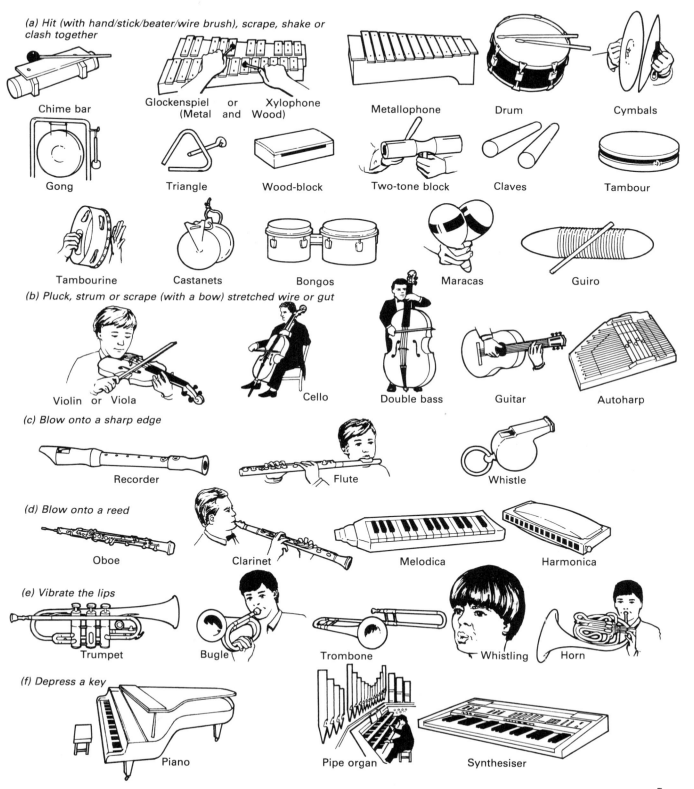

(a) Hit (with hand/stick/beater/wire brush), scrape, shake or clash together

Chime bar

Glockenspiel or Xylophone (Metal and Wood)

Metallophone

Drum

Cymbals

Gong

Triangle

Wood-block

Two-tone block

Claves

Tambour

Tambourine

Castanets

Bongos

Maracas

Guiro

(b) Pluck, strum or scrape (with a bow) stretched wire or gut

Violin or Viola

Cello

Double bass

Guitar

Autoharp

(c) Blow onto a sharp edge

Recorder

Flute

Whistle

(d) Blow onto a reed

Oboe

Clarinet

Melodica

Harmonica

(e) Vibrate the lips

Trumpet

Bugle

Trombone

Whistling

Horn

(f) Depress a key

Piano

Pipe organ

Synthesiser

5

Instruments and objects which have to be hit or plucked make either very short or fading sounds. This depends upon whether the vibrations die away quickly or slowly.

Usually boxes or tubes are fixed to the main vibrating parts. These 'catch' the vibrations and help them to last longer. They also give each type of instrument its familiar shape, as you can see on the previous page.

Fading sounds can always be cut short by pressing on the vibrating part to DAMP the vibrations or by playing again. Sounds on most other instruments can be both short or sustained until the player is tired or runs out of breath.

It will be more fun if as many pupils as possible play in the activities requiring instruments. Unless particular instruments are mentioned, there are usually several kinds that will do. These include any of your own as well as those called 'classroom' instruments, even those not completely suitable. For example, you may have to pretend that short-sound instruments (wood block, xylophone) are really making longer sounds. Remember, instruments like the tambourine can be shaken as well as hit.

Instrumental players can also join in the songs, playing either the song itself, when suitable, or an accompanying part. Later, you will all play these parts.

In your notebook

(ii) (Copy, completing the words)
Musical instruments and objects start vibrating in different ways. Many have to be h——, sh——, pl——, str—— or scr—— in order to make a part of them v——. Others are t—— of metal, plastic or wood, within which the air has to be set in vibration. This can be done by bl—— onto a sharp edge, onto a r—— —— or by making the l—— vibrate. It is possible to cut short fading sounds by pressing the vibrating part to d—— the v——.

Things to do

9. List the instruments in your classroom under the headings (a) to (f) given above. Most class instruments are type (a). Discuss where you would put the objects you used in 5 and 6.

10. Look at instruments of the various types brought by pupils or teacher. See the strings, sharp edges, reeds, etc, and watch as the instruments are played.

11. Each take a class instrument. Experiment with ways of starting and stopping the vibrations. Next, firmly touch different parts of it as you play. Does this ever affect the sound?

12. Take a fading-sound type (a) insrument. Experiment as follows:
(i) Work out where and how to hit for the best sound(s).
(ii) Hear the effect of using different beaters.
(iii) Hit with beater. Gently feel the vibrations.
(iv) Hit with beater but do not let it bounce off.
(v) Damp the vibrations in different ways, using finger or beater.
(vi) See what happens when a little salt is sprinkled onto the vibrating part.

13. Take a fading-sound type (a) instrument:
(a) All play simultaneously. Listen carefully to find whose sound is the last to fade away. Is the 'winner' the same if you hit (i) gently or (ii) hard?
(b) Again play. At a signal, damp the vibrations with your fingers (i) immediately and (ii) when you like.

14. Divide into two groups, using the above instruments. At a signal, the first group play a soft sound. When the last sound has faded away, the other group play a loud immediately damped sound as soon as possible. Immediately afterwards, the first group play again, and so on for an agreed number of times. Change groups.

15. Still use the same instruments and play chains as in 7. Either (a) overlap fading sounds or (b) damp immediately.

16. Decide on an order of playing unrelated to seating position and play chains as before. Use (a) objects as in 7 or (b) appropriate class or pupil instruments. It will now be necessary first to practise the chain slowly so that you can recognise the sound coming before yours. Later, play 'by ear' with eyes closed. Finally, reverse the order without any practice.

(a) Listen to recordings featuring instruments pictured on page 5. Identify (i) the type and (ii) the actual instrument.

2 SOUNDS DIFFERENT

Duration, pitch, volume

Composers use all the ways sounds can be different from each other to make their music suit the words or have the right mood. Before you sing this song, read the words and think about the kind of tune it ought to have. Space is saved by using

[1st time]   [2nd time] sections

‖:← − − −:‖− − − →

and repeat dots directing you back to the beginning or any facing dots.

'Flying Machines'

Here are the three most important ways sounds can be different from each other. As you read, you will hear sounds illustrating the differences. Sounds may be l o n g e r

or shorter

in DURATION

higher

OUR VOICES
HAVE NOT
BROKEN

or lower

MY
VOICE HAS
BROKEN

in PITCH

High notes seem
to come from here

Lower ones
from here

Not all musical instruments are PITCHED (TUNED or MELODIC). Some are UN-PITCHED (UNTUNED), having no recognisable NOTE that could be sung. Instead, they may make a jangle of different pitches or just an interesting sound. Many objects can also make musical pitched or unpitched sounds. Sounds may be louder or softer in VOLUME.

In your notebook

(i) (Copy, completing the words)
Musical sounds can be different from each other in several ways. They can be —— or —— in duration, —— or —— in pitch, —— or —— in volume.
A *murd* can only make short sounds, a *naipo* always fades away, a *lufte* can sustain a note until the player runs out of breath.
A *clamby* and *barmio tune* have no definite pitch, a *neopholyx* is a pitched instrument.
A *ben motor* and *gnog* are capable of both very loud and soft sounds, a *red corer* can only play rather quietly.
(The jumbled instruments are all on page 5)

Things to do

1. Move your arm up or down to match different pitches played to you.
2. Compare pairs of notes played on the same instrument. Which is (a) longer, (b) higher, (c) louder? Suggest how this can be made gradually more difficult in each case.
3. Compare the same pair of notes in two or more of the above ways.
4. Compare pairs of notes played on different instruments. Which is (a) longer and (b) higher?
5. Listen to several notes of the same pitch and one of another pitch, all played on different instruments. Spot the 'odd man out'.
6. Listen to groups of three sounds. Place in (a) duration, (b) volume and (c) pitch order.
7(a). Obey this sound code played on the piano: loud high note=stand; soft high note=arms up; loud low note=sit; soft low note=arms down.
Score + points for being the first to obey and − points for doing the wrong thing.
(b) Now modify or add to the code by including long and short sounds for other actions. This will be played on the glockenspiel(s), damping when necessary. Later, include the recognition of high, middle and low notes.

8

(c) Play 'Musical O'Grady'. For example, instructions after a high/higher pitch to be obeyed, those after a low/lower pitch to be ignored.

8. All sing the same pitch and try to memorise it. If you can still sing it at the end of the lesson (or in the next one) you may have the gift of pitch memory (absolute pitch).

9. Sign 'Flying Machines' again. What makes the tune suit the words so well? Name the film with a very similar theme song. Make up further verses and sing those voted the best.

Verses 2 and 3 could begin:
'The first airplanes were far too slow . . .'
'For what went up had down to come . . .'

10. Small groups take turns at making up (improvising) an extra accompaniment to the song. Use any class unpitched instruments and just let yourself go.

11. Watch what any pupil instrumentalists do when they (a) change pitch and (b) play the highest, lowest, longest, shortest, loudest and softest possible notes on their instrument.

12. Find out who can sing the highest, lowest, loudest and longest notes.

13. Now, who can remember that pitch?

(a) Listen to musical extracts featuring (i) very high and (ii) very low notes played by instruments pictured on page 5. Try to match the picture with each one.

Assignment

(A) Make a list of pieces (film/TV/pop music, etc.) where the tune matches the words or the mood in an interesting way. Bring records to play.

3 TALLEST ON THE LEFT

Instrument shapes and sizes

In Chapter 1 musical instruments were grouped according to what the player does to start the vibrations. It is possible to divide pitched instruments into just two groups. Here is one of the ways of doing it. Think about how it has been done:

Group A

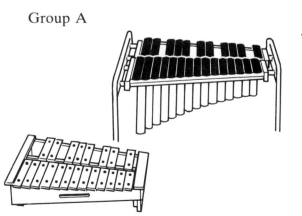

Group B

Things to do

1. Write down the names of A and B instruments without looking at Chapter 1.
2. Watch the pupils or teacher play some of the Group A instruments. Notice what each player does to change from high to low pitch. If possible, watch different-sized examples of the same instrument being played.
3. Similarly, see how different pitches are played on Group B instruments.
4. Listen to short recordings featuring instruments from both groups. Name each instrument and imagine it being played.

Now you can discuss what is the main difference between the groups.

Each instrument in Group A has a set of bars, strings or pipes giving fixed pitches. The player can choose from them but the pitches cannot normally be changed. With Group B instruments, however, the player has to get many pitches from just one tube or string. Look at the above pictures again. When you take the 'clothes' off Group A instruments you can see they all have a similar shape:

TALLEST PIPES ON THE LEFT!

You must also have noticed that the longer bars, strings and pipes on the left side of the player also produced the lower notes. This is why you can always expect large instruments to be generally lower in pitch than small ones of the same type. So tall instruments are also low!

In your notebook

(i) (Copy, unjumbling and completing the words)
Some instruments, like the *groan, gleelocksnip, raph* and *march bie*, have one or more fixed pitches. On these, the strings, pipes or bars are arranged so that the shorter, h—— pitched ones taper to the player's right. With all other pitched instruments, the player has to finger many notes from just one str—— or t—

Things to do

5. List the intruments in your classroom and brought by pupils under 'Unpitched', 'Fixed Pitch' and 'Player Makes Pitch'.
6. Pluck metal, gut (and possibly ordinary) strings. Hear the effect on pitch of:
(a) Using different lengths of the same string;
(b) Tightening or slackening the string;
(c) Using the same length of a different material;
(d) Using thicker strings of the same material.
(e) Changing the length of the vibrating part by pressing it with a finger or moving a raised 'bridge' under the string.
7. Hit bottles with a beater and then blow across the top. Is the pitch the same? Now add different amounts of water to the bottles.

8. Blow across the outlet of a bicycle pump while pushing in the plunger. Work out how to play a simple tune like 'Three Blind Mice'.

9. Hold the end of a ruler firmly and strike different parts of its edge against a table.

10. Hear what happens to the pitch of a chime bar when plasticine or a similar material is stuck on it. Discuss why some chime and glockenspiel bars may have notches cut underneath. Find out if metal and wooden bars of the same length sound the same pitch.

11. Now you can discuss all the things that affect the pitch of a string, bar or tube. Discuss particularly the effect on pitch of (a) increasing the tension of a string and (b) shortening a string or tube.

12. Stand in a line, each with a chime bar in descending pitch order. Play 'church bells'. Repeat for speed, timing each run.

Tuning up (and down)

We can now see what players of Type B instruments have to do to get different notes from just one string or tube. Although they cannot usually change the length of their instrument they can change the length of the part (a) that vibrates or (b) that encloses vibrating air.

Players of instruments such as the violin have the hardest job. First they tune each OPEN STRING to the correct pitch. Turning the peg so that it stretches the string gradually raises (SHARPENS) its pitch. Similarly, slackening the string gradually lowers (FLATTENS) its pitch.

Other notes can be obtained from each string by STOPPING a part of it from vibrating. This is done by pressing a finger at exactly the right place:

Guitar players are luckier. They have raised stopping places called FRETS to help them:

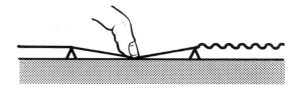

Instruments like the trumpet have extra pieces of tubing, PISTONS and VALVES:

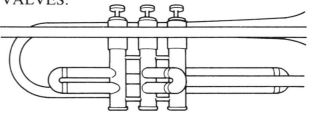

When the way ahead is blocked, diversions are always longer!

Trombones behave rather like a bicycle pump:

Many instruments, like the recorder, have holes that can be open or covered by the fingers:

Players of larger instruments have LEVERS and PADS to help them reach the holes:

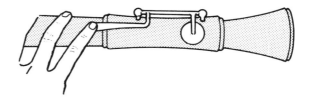

Things to do

13. Listen to the pitch getting sharper and flatter as the speed of a record is changed.

14. Listen and watch as a player tunes a violin or other string to the piano. Say whether the pitch of the string needs to be sharpened or flattened. Put up your hand when you think it is in tune. Do the same as any recorder players tune their instruments to the piano.

15. Watch players 'fingering' pairs of notes silently on both Type A and B instruments. Say which would have been the higher pitch.

16. Look at the pictures on page 11. Discuss how the various gadgets help the player change the instrument's vibrating length. Also examine them on any available Type B instruments. As they are played, hear the pitch change as fingers stop strings, cover holes or press pistons and levers, etc. Now discuss (a) why some violinists wobble their fingers on the strings and (b) why some tubes are in 'knots'.

In your notebook

(ii) (Copy, completing the words)
Even fixed pitch instruments can go out of tune. On these, if any note is too high, its string has to be sl—— or its tube made l——. This f—— the pitch. Doing the opposite sh—— the pitch.

Players of instruments like the v—— and double b——, when not playing o—— strings, have to make their own notes by st—— the vibrating length of the string with their f——. This shortens it and so sh—— the pitch. Guitarists have raised fr—— to make stopping the strings easier.

Players of instruments like the r——, tro——, tru—— and cl—— also have to make their own notes. Each has a different method of changing the length of vibrating air in their instrument.

---

4 THE TWO-FACED PIANO

The piano 'works' (action)

What kind of piano have you in your room? Is it tall and thin (UPRIGHT) or short and fat (GRAND) as shown on page 9? Every piano also has two faces. Its outside face (with shiny white and black teeth!) is very familiar. On page 9 they are shown 'undressed'. Now have a closer look inside:

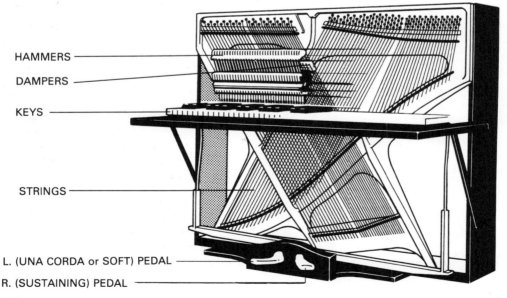

HAMMERS

DAMPERS

KEYS

STRINGS

L. (UNA CORDA or SOFT) PEDAL

R. (SUSTAINING) PEDAL

Things to do

1. Take any lid(s) and front covers off the class piano. What other instrument does the inside 'face' remind you of? When 'fully clothed', which shows the true inside shape of the instrument better—an upright or a grand? If possible, look at the inside 'works' of both as they are played. Discuss:

(a) Why the hammers bounce off the strings;
(b) What happens to the damper(s) when a key (i) goes down and (ii) comes up;
(c) What happens when the R. pedal is used;
(d) What happens when the L. pedal is used and the meaning of its Italian name;
(e) Why the lower strings are thicker;
(f) Why the higher notes have more than one string tuned to the same pitch;
(g) Which other page 5 group(s) the piano could be put in.

2. Take turns at making the piano strings vibrate in unusual ways: for example, with dampers both off and on, 'ping' the strings with the fingers. Feel the strings vibrating.

3. With the dampers off, compare the sustaining power of high and low notes.

The keyboard

Now, put the piano's clothes back on and have a closer look at its familiar shining face:

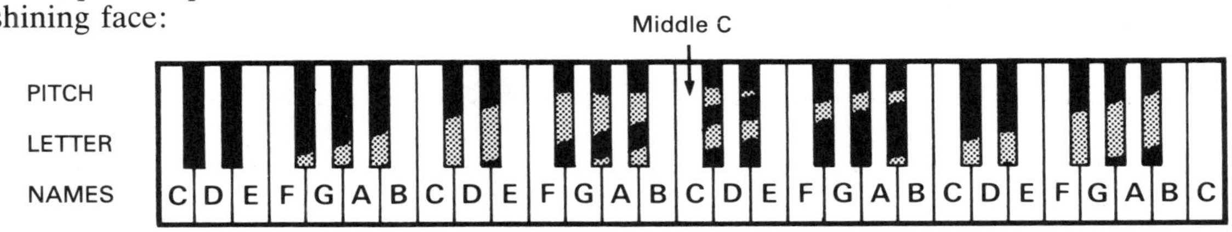

Other instruments, such as the organ and melodica, also have keyboards. Several classroom instruments have their keys arranged like a keyboard: Some have a part of the full pattern of 'black and white' keys:

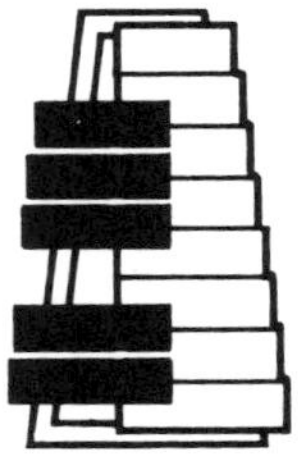

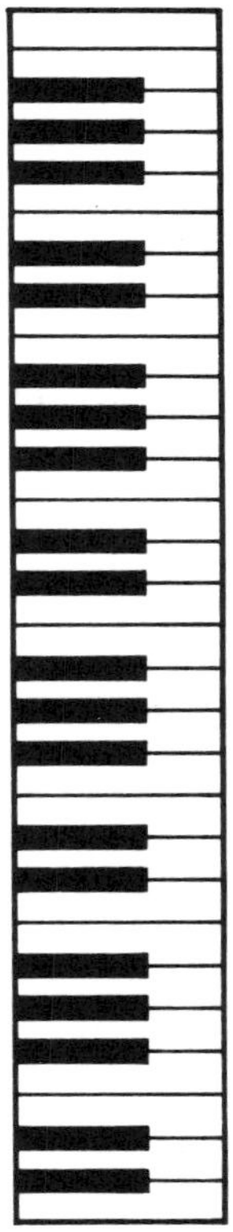

Others have only 'white' keys:

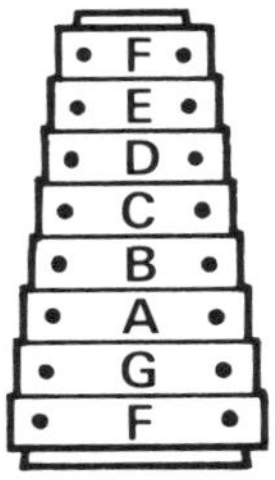

And some are single bars that can be used separately

or in a group:

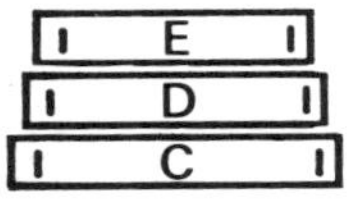

When there are no 'black' landmarks, each bar must have its letter name printed on it.

13

But 'landmarks' are much more useful than letters, even if you are not blind:

In most activities, letters may be played on a piano or any suitable classroom pitched instrument. The piano damps itself, but other fading-sound instruments may need to be damped if a note is not to be too long or overlap others. Later, when playing tunes, this damping will not usually be possible. Often, the piano and other large instruments can be shared by two or more pupils. Melodicas may also often be used, preferably on a stand.

The bars of most class instruments can be removed. Removing those not required can sometimes make playing easier.

Things to do

4. Remove all the bars from your classroom pitched instruments. See how long it takes you to replace them. You have both letters and sizes to help you.

5. Discuss ways of remembering where each letter fits in the keyboard pattern. You only need to remember one 'landmark' at first. The others can then be counted up or down from it.

6. Listen to the effect as four pupils play the same letter simultaneously on different parts of the piano keyboard. Repeat with different pupils and letters. When a mistake occurs, discuss why any 'odd men out' can be recognised.

7. Now listen as the same letter is played simultaneously on different instruments.

8. Sing the following songs:

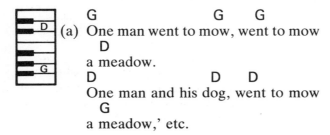

(a) 'One man went to mow, went to mow a meadow.
One man and his dog, went to mow a meadow,' etc.

(b) 'Ten green bottles hanging on the wall;
Ten green bottles hanging on the wall.
And if one green bottle should accidentally fall,
There'll be nine green bottles Hanging on the wall,' etc.

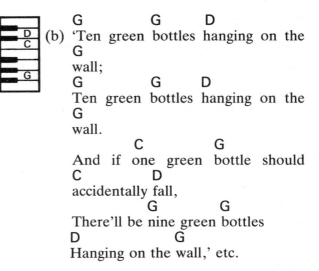

9. Now sing them again, clapping with the syllables that have letters over them. Finally, accompany a group of singers, playing the letters where you previously clapped:
(a) Each with just one note and playing when appropriate;
(b) Each playing all the notes required.
Remember to damp the vibrations or let the piano key come up just before any new letter sounds. Pitches may not mix yet.

10. In groups, work out where best to play notes G and D with the song 'Clementine'. When ready, play and sing to the class.

Octaves and unisons

Things to do

11. Set up an horizontal stretched 'string' or lay an instrument like a guitar, violin or cello carefully on a table. Using a 'bridge' or a finger to stop any string, hear what happens to the pitch when its vibrating length is exactly halved and quartered. E.g.

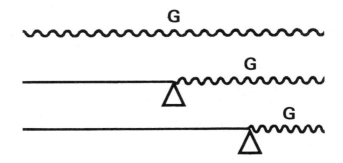

You have now discovered what Pythagoras first noticed in about the year 550 B.C. Halving the length of a string always produces a note higher than, yet strangely similar to, that of its full length. We say that this note is an OCTAVE above, and give it the same letter name. Further halving of the string will produce the next octave above, and so on.

The same arithmetic also applies to the vibrating air in a tube and to vibrating bars of metal and wood.

When men sing the same tune with women or boys with unbroken voices they adjust to an octave lower automatically.

Similarly, as class pitched instruments are made in different sizes, you will often be mixing different octaves together. This will not usually matter. Notes sung or played that are *exactly* the same are said to be in UNISON.

In your notebook

(i) (Copy, completing the words)
When different people sing or play identical notes they are in u——. Higher and lower notes with a very similar sound are called o—— and have the same l—— name. A higher o—— can be obtained by halving the length of a str——, tube or bar. A lower octave is then obtained by d—— its length. This is why each letter can be repeated many times and always occupies the same position in the k—— pattern.

Things to do

12. Draw a rough keyboard in two stages:

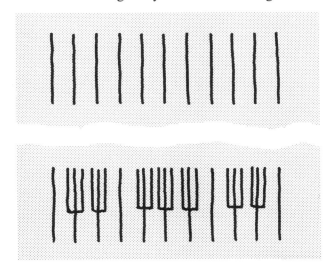

Now, write one of the following words on the correct keys: CAD, DEAD, FADE, DACE (all L. to R.). Volunteers play their word at any octave on the piano (also L. to R.). Identify the word each time. Discuss:
(a) Why the piano keys are not lettered A to Z;
(b) Why the keyboard is not

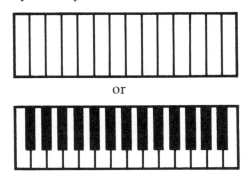

or

(c) Why there are names on chime bars but not on the piano keys;
(d) Why 'octave' is often shortened to '8ve'.
13. Make a list of other words/phrases using the letters A to G, starting with A BAD EGG, CABBAGE. Can you think of any more with seven or more letters?
14. Now all play the words in 13. Play each note when directed and point to 'odd men out'.
15. Hear the same letter at different 8ves (a) on the piano and (b) on different instruments. Identify the highest and lowest 8ves. Now sing an 8ve above and below given notes. Which is harder?
16. Recognise simple tunes played on the piano with each note at the wrong 8ve.
17. Find out the letter name of the highest and lowest notes, together with the number of octaves on all your instruments with keyboards. Apart from the piano, which of them can sound the (a) highest, (b) lowest note?
18. Hear the same pitch played on the piano and other instruments. Discuss why you can tell one instrument from another.
19. Each play a note in succession and identify the highest and lowest pitches. Repeat, calling out 'snap' if you think successive notes are in unison or 8ves. Score + points for the first correct challenges and − points for false alarms.
20. Play Musical Bingo. You will each be allocated one letter from a choice of four. Make yourself familiar with its pitch and play if you think the 'caller' at the piano matches your letter. Score as above. Repeat, first changing your notes, and then with a wider choice.

5 SECRET CODES

Why we need codes

Did you realise that the words you are now reading are a code?

We need codes to help us remember, or communicate anything—even music. See what happens when we must do without them.

Things to do

1. Pass a short message around the class by whispering it from person to person. For fun, vary it by (a) passing the message in separate word 'helpings', (b) passing two separate messages simultaneously in opposite directions and (c) having a race, passing the same message round two equal teams. Do the messages change?

2. Decide on a category such as football teams, flowers, etc. The first person says a name in that category (for example, Leeds, rose, etc.) and each person in turns says the word(s) already used and adds a further one. Those who forget or make a mistake drop out, leaving the winner at the end.

3. Echo back very short tunes played to you.

4. Choose about five pupils who do not mind singing on their own to stand outside the door. The first enters and hears a short unknown tune. The second pupil now enters and hears the tune sung by the first. Repeat until the last pupil has sung to the class. Did the tune gradually change? What has this game got to do with the folk-song you are about to sing?

A folk song from Wales: 'The Golden Wheat'

1. A young and fool - ish lad am I, I go where fan - cy leads me. ___ I
2. O tell me tru - ly, gen - tle Ann, O tru - ly give your an - swer. ___ Will

stand and guard the gold - en wheat, a - no - ther does the reap - ing. ___ The
you be mine for e - ver-more or do you love a - no - ther? ___ Un -

wind blows col - der day by day and you grow e - ver fair - er. ___ Sep -
- til the salt dries in the sea and whilst my eyes can seek you, ___ Un -

- tem - ber comes and I must go, will you not fol - low af - ter? ___
- til my heart dies in my breast, I'll sure - ly, sure - ly, love you. ___

16

You can now see why any folk-song you sing may well have changed a great deal from the original version. Music that is not written down when it is composed is liable to get changed over the years. This was particularly true before radio and recording. It is also likely to change as it spreads from one part of the country to another. If you want to remember music or any other kind of message, you must have a written code or language of some kind. People never seem to get spoken messages right!

Here is an example of a musical code that has been used in the Navy since the Middle Ages. This particular one reminds the bosun how to play Dinner Call on his pipe:

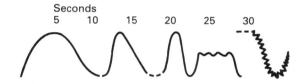

Can you guess what it sounds like?

The code gives the player a rough idea of the two most important things about any note. Think about what they are.

Things to do

5. Groups take turns at accompanying the above song, adding C, F and G where indicated over the words. Now what are those two things?

A proper musical code must tell you (a) what note to play and (b) how long (and when) to play it.

Fitting letters against words is cheating really. Besides, unlike the bosun's code, it gives you no idea of notes going up and down in pitch.

A simple music code

Things to do

6. Pretend that no musical codes have ever been invented. Now make up your own to show differences in (a) pitch, (b) duration and (c) volume as pairs of notes are played to you. Did anybody make their code read from right to left? Could a musician now read your codes and play the notes exactly as you heard them?

Most music needs a really exact code, especially for showing differences in pitch and duration. However, it can be fun to learn a simpler code as well. This will enable you to make the sort of music quite common today, where these things need to be less exact.

Players of instruments will now have no advantage. You are not only going to learn a new code but you may obtain your sounds from both instruments and other objects in any way you please:

A single short sound, either produced naturally or immediately damped on a fading-sound instrument.

A single sound on a fading-sound instrument that is allowed to fade naturally.

A single fading sound, damped when you choose or at a given point.

A very quickly repeated sound, or TREMOLO, on any kind of instrument, ending when you choose or at a given point.

f

Loudly (the Italian for loud is *forte*—pronounced 'fortay').

p

Softly (the Italian for soft is *piano*—pronounced 'peearno').

Remember:

(a) Most instruments and objects can make both long or fading sounds and short ones. Unless told otherwise, do any damping quietly with a finger.

(b) Some instruments can only play short sounds.

(c) The duration of both sounds and silences must approximately match the spacing of any code.

(d) The importance of absolute silence before playing, during 'rests' and at the end.

(e) Play at a moderate volume, unless any conductor gestures otherwise, or *f* and *p* are indicated. These signs keep their effect until cancelled.

Things to do

7. For a start we will do without a code at all. Take any pitched or unpitched class instrument and each choose to play one of the following sound patterns that suits it:

(a) Fast sounds gradually slowing down to a stop;

(b) Slow sounds gradually getting faster, stopping when the limit is reached;

(c) Loud slow sounds getting softer until nothing can be heard;

(d) Four fast loud sounds and, after a gap, four very slow soft sounds;

(e) Ten alternately loud and soft slow sounds.

  Now all play, starting (i) together or (ii) when you like, Repeat, changing both instrument and pattern.

8. Take any instrument and sit in a large circle with a conductor in the middle. Play a short medium-loud sound (damping if necessary) when the conductor points at you or swings an arm round. Repeat, playing loudly or softly according to the conductor's gestures. Take turns at being conductor.

9. On appropriate pitched or unpitched instruments, all play a single ● ●⌒ ●⌐ or ⋁⋁ as requested. Start, stop or damp when the conductor indicates. Watch carefully and repeat until all respond exactly together. Take turns at being conductor and change instruments.

  Next, play loudly or softly according to the conductor's gestures.

10. Choose any short-sound instruments. Following the conductor for your starts and stops, play the following:

● ● ⋁⋁⋁⋁ ● ⋁⋁ ⋁⋁⋁⋁ ● ●

Repeat, this time each starting when you like. Now use fading-sound pitched or unpitched in-

struments and damp immediately.

11. First play the following parts as in 10:

(a) ● ⋁⋁ ● ⋁⋁⋁⋁ ● ⋁⋁ ⋁⋁

(b) ⋁⋁⋁⋁ ● ⋁⋁⋁⋁ ● ● ●

Now, get into two groups using contrasted instruments. For example:

(a) wood pitched pitches C, F or G   fading
    or   or   or   or
(b) metal unpitched pitches D E or A   short

Play the two parts damping if necessary and not starting together, (a) under two conductors and (b) all making your sounds when you think you should. Think of other ways of doing this.

12. All take a chime bar or share a glockenspiel or metallophone. Each decide whether to damp instantly or after about two, five or ten seconds. Play together and listen to the effect. Repeat, changing your note-duration every time.

13. Using fading pitched or unpitched instrument, practise the following under various conductors. Make sure there are no sounds after you have damped your note:

(a) ● ●⌒ ●⌐ ● ● ●⌒

(b) ● ●⌐ ● ●⌒ ● ● ● ●⌒ ●

Now, in two groups and with contrasted fading-sound instruments, play the parts together as in 11.

14. First play the following parts separately under a conductor, obeying the *f* and *p* instructions. Use suitable instruments for each one.

(a) A ● ● ● ⋁⋁⋁ ⋁⋁ ●
      f   *p* *f* *p*   *f*

(b) B ● ● ⋁⋁⋁ ⋁⋁ ● ● ● ⋁⋁
      p   *f*   *p* *f p*   *f p*

(c) C ⋁⋁ ●⌒ ● ⋁⋁⋁ ●⌒
      p   *f* *p*   *f* *p*

(d) D ⋁ ●⌐●⌒⌐ ● ⋁⋁⋁⋁
      f   *f p f*   *p*

(e) E ●⌐ ⋁⋁⋁⋁⋁ ⋁⋁ ● ●⌒
      p   *f*   *p*

(f) F ● ● ● ● ⋁ ⋁ ●⌒●
      p f p *f p f*   *f*

(g) G ⋁⋁⋁⋁⋁⋁ ⋁⋁ ●⌐⋁ ●⌒ ⋁⋁ ●
      p   *f*   *p* *f* *p*

Repeat without a conductor so that you now no longer all play together.

Next, in two or more groups, mix any of the parts under different conductors, and later without conductors. Use (i) any appropriate contrasting pitched or unpitched instruments or objects or (ii) any pitched instruments and play the letter indicated for each part.

Finally, in groups of seven, experiment with other instrumental contrasts and perform to the rest of the class. Criticise each performance and vote for the best.

15. Each choose an instrument and write a part for it similar to those in 14. All play simultaneously or in groups in various ways.

16. Listen to (a) single sounds, (b) two sounds and (c) several unequally spaced sounds. Write them down in the above code (include *f* and *p*).

6 AS REGULAR AS CLOCKWORK

Pulse, tempo, rhythm

 (a) Listen to tracks from pop records/cassettes. What do you notice others doing as they listen? Now, if you wish, pretend you are at a disco.

Look at the pictures on pages 23–4. Several of these also show people moving to music in some way. Music not only often makes us want to move, it also makes some working movements easier—and even fun. It is usually even more enjoyable if they are done 'in step' with others and at a regular speed.

This is why dancing has always been so popular. As we enjoy making and watching regular movements so much it is not surprising we often get the urge to move in time to the music we listen to. Movements and music are such close friends. No wonder most music for singing and listening, as well as dance music, also moves along regularly like an engine or clock—so unlike the music you made on page 18.

The steady tick of the musical clock is called the BEAT or PULSE. It may go at any speed(s) or TEMPO (TEMPI) the performer wishes.

In 1, you discovered that some of the notes of the song were beat-length ones and fitted exactly against the song's engine or beat. Others, however, were longer or shorter than the beat. Most music, except some simple hymns or songs, has this mixture of different note-lengths. It is what you can clap, and is called the RHYTHM. As a clap can only make a short sound, we have to cheat by holding the hands together for longer notes.

In your notebook

(i) (Copy, completing the words)
Most music has a regular background b—— or p—— running through it. The longer the duration of the b—— the slower the te——. The mixture of different note-lengths that can be clapped is called the r——. Music, just like most machines, usually keeps going at the same te—— once it has started, perhaps slowing down at the end.
(ii) List as many activities as you can in which music accompanies regular movements. Use the pictures on pages 23 and 24 to give you a start.
(iii) Many non-musical things in our lives also happen regularly. Solve the jumbled answers, and then list as many more as you can: *hater bate, yad nad thing,*

Things to do

1. First sing any well-known song. Now sing again, one group clapping regularly with the song's 'engine', the other with each syllable. Finally, look at each other as you clap while singing the song in your head.

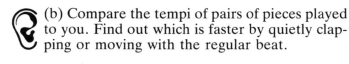 (b) Compare the tempi of pairs of pieces played to you. Find out which is faster by quietly clapping or moving with the regular beat.

You would expect a song about a clock to have a strong regular beat. In the next song (and a later one) notice more space-saving signs:

D.S. go back to 𝄋
(Italian: 'dal segno') } and end
D.C. go back to the } at FINE
beginning (pron. 'feenay')
(Italian: 'da capo')

'My Grandfather's Clock'

Things to do

2. Listen to the melodic/class instruments part played. Does it remind you of anything?

3. Sing the song again and add one or more of the following accompaniments:

(a) A regular 'tick tock' on a two-tone block;

(b) An improvised tambourine part.

4. Now sing verse 1, clapping with its rhythm. Next, clap the rhythm while silently 'singing' in your head. Finally, clap the regular 'tick tock' while singing the song in your head. Keep at the same speed and suddenly stop with an extra loud clap at the word 'died'.

5. Divide into two groups. One group clap with the song's rhythm and the other with the regular beat. Still sing in your head, fit together, and again stop at 'died'.

6. Try to clap with the beat while the piano is played at a constantly changing tempo. When you get the chance, try walking or running while changing your speed every few steps!

7. Clap or play unpitched instruments at a given tempo. What happens when music at a different tempo is played?

8. Decide 'privately' at which tempo to clap or play. At a signal, start together. What happens?

9. Again clap with the regular beat while singing 'My Grandfather's Clock'. How many beats are silent ones?

10. Sing the song, this time only singing aloud on alternate claps, beginning: 'My grand—— clock—— tall', etc.

11. Repeatedly sing the first line, cutting one word off the end each time. Silently imagine what you would have sung in the increasing gaps.

12. All start to sing verse 1. At a signal, stop singing aloud but keep going 'in your head'. Clap (or sing the word at the correct pitch) when you reach 'died'. If you were not together, suggest how you can keep the beat going 'as regular as clockwork'. Now see what happens when you repeat this, keeping as still as possible during the silent singing.

13. Set up a pendulum (or metronome) that all can see swinging.

Now sing verse 2, keeping in time with its swing. Repeat at different tempi. What do you have to do to the pendulum to change its speed of swing?

14. Take turns at tapping the rhythm of a well-known song to be recognised by the others. First correct answers score + points and wrong ones − points. Award bonus points for suc-cessful challenges to any inaccurate rhythms.

15. Using hit instruments or clapping, echo back short rhythms played to you.

16. Repeat Chapter 2, 7, but this time using a rhythm code. Start the game when you think you can remember the four rhythms.

17. Clap the following rhythms against a regular 'tick tock':

(a) 'Grandfather's clock was too tall for the shelf'

(b) 'Stopped, short, never to go again'

Now, in two groups, repeat each one together, singing the words in your head as you clap.

18. Repeat 17, using contrasted unpitched instruments for each group. For example:

hit metal   or   tambourines
hit wood   drums

Now play while 'My Grandfather's clock' is played on the piano. How many times did you have to repeat each rhythm? Finally, sing the song as two pupils add the rhythms as an accompaniment.

19. Take or share an instrument capable of playing one of the following words:

ACE, AGE, CAD, CAGE, AGED, DACE.

Using one or two beaters, improvise on the notes in any order, repeating them if necessary. Use the rhythm of one of these song-openings:

(a) 'Three Blind Mice';

(b) 'My Old Man's a Dustman'.

Take turns at playing your pattern to the class four times in succession. Then two pupils combine one of each rhythm. Finally, all play simultaneously.

Crotchets and quavers

Using rhythms from songs is cheating really. You cannot write and play new rhythms until you learn the proper code. This is much more exact than the ones used in Chapter 5.

Here is the beginning of rhythm 17 (a) showing how the notes fit against the background 'tick tock'. Notice how syllables are separated by hyphens:

'grand-fa-ther's clock'
tick   tock   tick

The note lasting for one beat, ♩ or ⌐ , is called a CROTCHET.
The two shorter half-beat notes that fit against it ♫ are called QUAVERS.

'Junior's legs have to go twice as fast to keep up with Dad'

Single quavers ♪ have no 'hand' to hold.

In rhythm 17 (b) the clock appears to miss two 'tocks':

♩ 𝄽 ♩ 𝄽
'stopped short'
tick tock tick tock

The sign for one beat's silence, 𝄽 or ⌐ , is called a CROTCHET REST.

When clapping a rhythm, hold your hands apart, and 'nod' each beat during rests.

It is a pity that the written symbols, the piano keys and instrument bars are also often called 'notes'. Strictly speaking, only the sounds are notes!

In your notebook

(iv) Draw and label the following: crotchet, crotchet rest, two quavers.
(v) Now write a row of four crotchets and then four pairs of quavers underneath, showing how they fit against each other.

Things to do

20. In two groups, clap crotchets against quavers, saying 'grand' or 'father' with the claps. At a signal, change note values. Repeat, just clapping.

21. The extracted rhythms from the song can also fit exactly against each other:

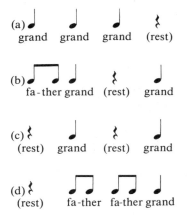

Repeatedly clap each one separately, and then combine in groups.

22. Here are some more four-beat rhythm patterns:

(a) ♩ ♩ ♩ 𝄽
grand grand grand (rest)

(b) ♫ ♩ 𝄽 ♩
fa-ther grand (rest) grand

(c) 𝄽 ♩ 𝄽 ♩
(rest) grand (rest) grand

(d) 𝄽 ♫ ♫ ♩
(rest) fa-ther fa-ther grand

Repeat each one four times, (i) just saying 'grand', 'father' or 'rest', (ii) clapping and saying these words and (iii) just clapping. Nod your head and say 'rest' in your head during the silences.

Now, in four groups, using contrasted un-pitched instruments, combine the patterns as an accompaniment to 'My Grandfather's Clock' and 'Flying Machines' played on the piano. How many times did you have to repeat them?

Finally, four pupils accompany the singing of both these songs.

23. Compose four more four-beat patterns, using only the above values. Again set them out like an addition sum, but without the words. Each choose one of their rhythms and combine as in 22. If necessary, say the rhythm words in your head as you play.

24. Identify the letter as the following are played separately in any order.

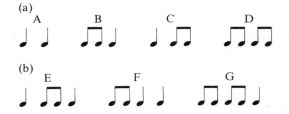

Now identify the word(s) made as several are played in quite close succession. Select first from (a) and then (a) and (b) mixed.

25. Write down four-beat rhythm patterns tapped on an unpitched wooden instrument.

26. Repeat some of the above at different tempi. Try also singing the song and clapping a rhythm pattern at the same time.

27. Gently clap the beats as you 'sing' verse 1 of 'My Grandfather's Clock' in your head. Count how many beats there are between the words 'clock' and 'stood' (inclusive).

28. As many as possible practise playing the following two notes on any class pitched instrument:

G A G G G A G G G A G G G A G G
G G G A G G A A G A G A G A G G
G G G G G G G G G A G A G A G

At first, play each one when directed. Then play every two beats. Finally, repeat as an accompaniment to the song played on the piano.

29. Now, do the same with these four notes:

D C B C D C B B B C B C D C B B
B B C D D E D D D C D E D C B B
D B D D D B D D D D D C D C B

30. Repeat 3, adding both 28 and 29 to the accompaniment.

7 MUSIC WHILE YOU WORK

The uses of music

(a) Listen to music associated with some of the following pictures. Match picture to music. Which country does each picture remind you of? Does any of it sound strange?

(e) (f)

(a) (b)
(c)
(d)

You need no reminding that there is a lot of music about today. It is the same all over the world. In fact, people everywhere have always enjoyed or used music. Musical instruments can be seen in ancient cave paintings, and are mentioned in the Bible. The Greeks of about 400 BC thought that music affected character—and we are told that the Roman emperor Nero fiddled while Rome burned!

The very first music must have been associated with movement—perhaps in a communal work-activity or ritual dance round a camp fire. Nobody knows what really ancient music sounded like, so we can never hear a recording of it. If we could go back thousands of years we would probably think the music very odd—just as some music from other parts of the world today sounds strange to us.

The pictures on the next page show some of the ways music has been used down the ages:

In your notebook

(i) (Copy, using pictures (a)-(j) to help you unjumble the words)

Long ago, music was always 'do it yourself' and not listened to at concerts. *Flok* singers were popular and so was *canding*, but much music was used to make *krowing* more pleasant, and this still happens today in some parts of the world. Music can even be used to send *gassemes* or *march skanes*.

Things to do

1. List what the music is being used for in pictures (a)-(j). About how long ago do you think such music-making took place in pictures (g)-(j)? Which example would have sounded the most strange to us today?

2. The unusual instruments shown in some of the pictures (a)-(j) are rather like the more familiar ones named in Chapter 1. Match pictures to instrument(s).

Here is a working song. The solos would have been sung by the shantyman and the choruses by the sailors as they hauled in the sails. It was the job of the shantyman to improvise new verses to keep them working happily. Verses about the ship's officers, bad food and girl-friends were among the most popular:

A sea shanty: 'Haul away Joe'

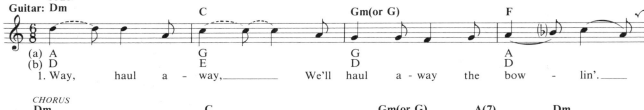

Things to do

3. Choose a shantyman to sing the solo and have the chorus haul imaginary sails as they sing. Repeat at different speeds. Now make up new words about your teacher, other pupils, homework, music lessons or your school. Sing those voted the best.

Intervals

(b) Listen to (i) more music from other parts of the world, trying to guess where it comes from and (ii) music written many hundreds of years ago. Discuss what clues helped tell you it was old music or from another part of the world.

Many things give any music its particular sound and help us to guess where it comes from or when it was written. You might have mentioned its rhythm, the type of tune or the sound of unusual instruments or voices. Some Indian and other music even uses extra pitches that would come in the 'cracks' between the keys on our keyboards.

The way the notes are mixed is also an important clue. The 'flavour' of two notes played together depends upon how far they are apart, or their INTERVAL.

Intervals are measured like this:

'Next-door' notes .... are 2nds

'Next-door-but-one' notes .... are 3rds

Notes 'three doors away' .... are 4ths

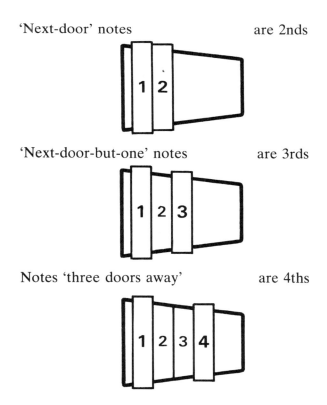

and so on. You could use your fingers to measure intervals, and to work out how many 2nds, 3rds or 4ths there are on a piano:

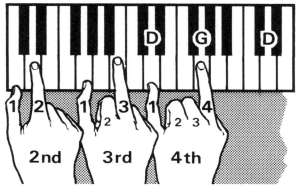

As octaves share the same 'family' sound, reversing or INVERTING the two letters of any interval does not make much difference to the sound mixture. It changes its name, though. For example, a 4th becomes a 5th:

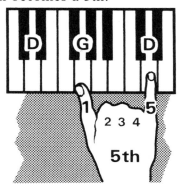

Things to do

4. Using only the white keys, find out how many 2nds, 3rds, 4ths and octaves could be played (a) on the first piano above and (b) on the various instruments with a keyboard pattern in your room.

What is odd about the way we measure musical distances compared with normal distances or the interval of a concert? Work out another name for an octave. Although the unison is not really an interval, what else could it be called?

Letting the last illustration help you, what do 2nds and 3rds become when the two notes are inverted?

5. Use any suitable instruments and experiment to find the differences in 'flavour' between 2nds, 3rds, 4ths and octaves when played together. Also prove that 2nds sound rather like 7ths, and so on.

6. Recognise whether interval mixtures played to you are (a) 2nds or 3rds, (b) 3rds or 4ths, (c) 3rds or octaves or (d) any combination of these.

7. Hear rows of 2nds, 3rds, 4ths or 8ves played

like tunes on the piano. Identify each interval.

You should have less trouble recognising them now, as playing them this way seems to strengthen each particular 'flavour'. Discuss the sort of music each interval reminds you of. Also choose words from (iii) below to suit them.

8. Use two beaters to play rows of 2nds, 3rds or 4ths on any instrument with a keyboard pattern, listening to the different effects. If you remember to keep your fingers or beaters the same distance apart you should find this quite easy.

In your notebook

(ii) (Copy, completing the words)
The distance between two notes is called an i——. I—— are measured by counting both their first and last letters and any letters between. For example, n—— – d—— notes are called 2nds and o—— may also be called 8ths.

(iii) Copy, rearranging the items in columns two and three to match the sound of the interval mixture.

Interval	'Flavour'	Type of music
2nd	pleasant	'oriental'
3rd	bare	'modern'
4th	clashing	'normal'

A song from the Orient: 'Miya Sama, Miya Sama'

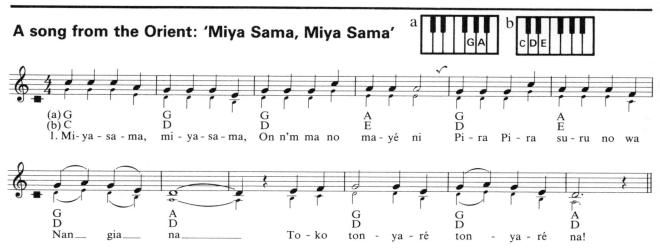

(a) G   G   G   A   G   A
(b) C   D   D   E   D   E
1. Mi- ya - sa - ma, mi - ya-sa-ma, On n'm ma no ma - yé ni Pi - ra Pi - ra su - ru no wa

G   A   G   G   A
D   D   D   D   D
Nan__ gia__ na__ To - ko ton - ya - ré ton - ya - ré na!

(c) Listen to the above song, as it appears in Gilbert and Sullivan's *The Mikado*. Try singing with the recording.

Things to do

9. Use suitable class pitched instruments to practise parts (a) and (b) above. Then, in two groups, play them together. Listen to the oriental effects of the 5ths (or 4ths, depending on which 8ves are used). Now sing again, several players adding the above accompaniment. Change notes (and damp) with the correct syllables as before.
10. Repeat 9 with a second group singing a 4th below the tune (small notes).
11. Make up English words to fit this tune. Sing the best verses.
12. Similarly, practise the parts given with 'Haul Away Joe' and then accompany the singing.

Assignments

(A) List examples of music or its effects playing an important part in legends, ancient stories, the Bible and history books. Add any interesting or unusual effects caused by music today.
(B) Do you know the names of any old or foreign instruments? Although the translators had to use names people would understand, what instruments are mentioned in the Bible? Have you heard any old instruments at a concert or on television—or seen any in a museum? Some 'pop' artists use unusual instruments. Can you name any players and their instruments? Bring appropriate records/cassettes to play.

26

8 FASHIONS AND RECIPES

Mixing rhythms

Things to do

1. Repeat Chapter 6, 11. What did you find yourself doing during the gaps? As you use the following rhythms, also 'sing' the words to yourself or 'nod' the silent beats:

Z   Y
'Grand-fa-ther's clock was too tall   for the shelf'
X
'stopped   short   nev-er to go   a-gain'

(beats)

At the same tempo:
(a) Clap the rhythms separately.
(b) In two groups, clap the rhythms against each other four times. Fit with the beats as indicated.
(c) Repeat the rhythms in succession four times.
(d) Get into two groups with contrasted unpitched instruments. Play the two rhythms as (c) but with the second group delaying its start until the first has reached X, Y or Z.
2. Use the different methods of 1, separately or together, as an accompaniment to 'My Grandfather's Clock' and 'Flying Machines'. Repeat each pattern the necessary number of times.
3. Now treat these rhythms as in 1 and 2:

Z   Y
'Jin-gle bells, jin-gle bells,   jin-gle all the way'
X
'Ten green bot-tles   hang-ing on the wall'

(beats)

4. In four groups, using contrasted unpitched instruments, combine the four rhythms of 1 and 3. Play each rhythm eight times. Finally, four pupils take turns at repeating these patterns as an accompaniment to the songs.
5. Repeat the delayed-start activities of 1 and 3,

each with four groups. At first delay until X. Later try Y and Z.
6. First repeat Chapter 6, 22.
Next clap the patterns in immediate succession. Now, in two groups, perform with a delayed start, the second group beginning when the first group starts the second pattern. This is what you have just done:

Finally, in two or more groups and using contrasted unpitched instruments, delay the starts until X, Y or Z. Still say 'grand', 'father' or 'rest' in your head if necessary. Is it possible to tell at the end if your group has gone wrong?
7. First write the following in succession as above. Again repeat it underneath with a similar delayed start. Then perform in all the ways described in 6:

8. Clap these rhythms in succession. Then, in two or more groups, perform then with delayed starts as above:

Z   Y
'I've got a lovely bunch of coconuts'
X
'Oh, dear! What can the matter be. Oh, dear! What can the matter be'

9. Repeat Chapter 6, 19. Use the same rhythms with the following words:
BAG, DAB, AGE, AGED, BEAD, BADGE.
Now similarly use the rhythms from 3 and 8 above, played four times. Combine as before.

A thirteenth-century song: 'Sumer is icumen in'

Sum - mer is a - com - ing in,___ Loud - ly sing, Cuck - oo! Grow - eth seed, And blow - eth mead, And spring - eth wood a - new; Sing Cuck - oo! Ewe___ bleat - eth af - ter lamb, Low'th af - ter calf the cow, Bul - lock start - eth, buck de - part - eth, Mer - ry sing, Cuck - oo! Cuck - oo! Cuck - oo!___ Well sing'st thou Cuck - oo!___ Nor cease to sing___ now.

Second Part
Sing Cuck - oo! now,_ Sing Cuck - oo!

Things to do

10. As many as possible take turns at playing this 5th, using two beaters:

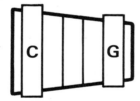

Repeat every two beats. Now add these accompaniments to the song:
(a) The above repeated 5th.
(b) The rhythms of 8, repeated and played on wood block and drum respectively.

Ostinato, round, drone

Fashions are always changing. Whatever it is, there comes a time when people want to make or do things differently. This is either because they think they have found a better way, or they just want a change. Think how frequently fashions change in pop music! Perhaps you have also noticed that the 'wheel of fashion' often turns full circle.

For example, beards, long hair and short dresses have a habit of coming back:

The sort of music composers write has also changed many times over the centuries. The 'recipes' they use, the sound mixtures they like and even the instruments have never been exactly the same for long, as you can see on page 29.

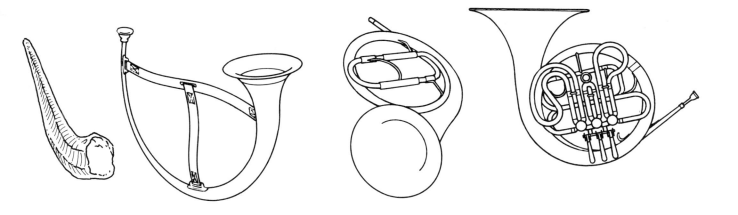

Many hundreds of years ago, composers started experimenting with musical patterns. They began with:

the PHRASE: The shortest group of notes (or words) that makes sense on its own. Did you notice in 1 how you felt that you wanted to finish the incomplete phrases? Most TUNES (MELODIES) consist of several phrases.

Then they looked for ways of making their music longer or more interesting. Several useful 'recipes' invented long ago have been used on and off ever since. You have recently been experimenting with them yourselves:

OSTINATO: The constant repetition of one or more melodic or rhythmic phrases, often as an accompaniment to a longer melody.

ROUND or CANON: The same tune or rhythm performed by two or more groups with delayed starts.

DRONE: One or more notes, usually low, played or repeated continuously throughout a piece. Bagpipes always play a drone note.

In your notebook

(i) (Copy, completing the words)
An o——— is the repetition of a phr——— throughout a piece. When the same t——— is repeated by two or more groups with delayed starts it is called a r——— or c———. A dr——— is a continuous low note used as an accompaniment.

(a) Listen to a recording of 'Sumer is icumen in'. You will hear that it is a round with an additional sung ostinato accompaniment. Also hear other examples of the above 'recipes' in both ancient and more modern musical 'fashions'.

Things to do

11. Now you sing the song on page 28 as a round in two to four parts. X_1 shows the delaying point. Next, learn the Second Part, repeating it as an ostinato. This can also then be sung as a round from X_2. Finally, mix it all together with the double drone and rhythmic ostinati of 8 and 10.

12. In groups, experiment to find two or more song-opening rhythms that fit against each other, as in 8. Perform as before.

13. See how many words you can make using any of the letters C D E G A one or more times. Each choose one to play on any pitched instrument. Play it in any rhythm, repeating the pattern as an ostinato against a background beat. Now all start your ostinati (a) in a planned sequence or (b) when you like.

William I	Henry I	John	Henry III	Edward II	Edward III	Henry V
BATTLE OF HASTINGS	THE CRUSADES			Simon de Montfort	Black Prince	AGINCOURT
DOMESDAY BOOK	St Francis		MODEL PARLIAMENT		PEASANTS' REVOLT	Joan of Arc
			BANNOCKBURN			

9 THE MIDDLE AGES

As we can know so little about really ancient musical 'fashions', our journey from the past begins with the Middle Ages. The Medieval Period, as it is also called, stretches from the 'Dark Ages' to the beginning of the modern world in the fifteenth century. They are called the 'Dark Ages' because we know so little about them. The Middle Ages, however, includes the above famous people and events—from William the Conqueror to Henry V and Agincourt. Although there were no music colleges (or music teachers!), orchestras or concerts, there was plenty of music about.

30

In churches, where an early type of organ was the only instrument allowed, choirs were needed to sing the Latin words of the services and the often complicated music. At court and in the houses of the nobility, simple short pieces were played for entertainment or dancing, while wandering minstrels sang for both rich and poor. On the Continent these were called TROUBADOURS, and they were often men of noble birth—Richard the Lion-Heart being one.

Generally, however, 'gentlemen' (and ladies) only sang and played in private. It would not have done for the common people to have seen them!

Early music

Composers did not usually care which instruments played their pieces and were only just beginning to invent ways of writing their music down. As you can see, their first codes looked more like the shorthand that secretaries use today, and were only used to jog the performer's memory.

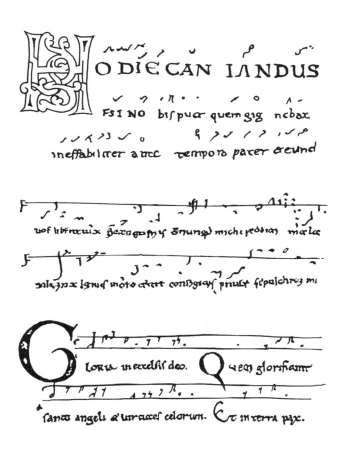

This is the original manuscript of the song you sang on page 28. Compare the two codes

It took many centuries of change to arrive at the code normally used today. Much music was never written down, and the different versions of today's folk-songs are the result of an old tune being passed by memory from person to person.

During the Middle Ages, composers became interested in mixing different pitches together for the first time. Their favourite intervals were the 'oriental' and bare-sounding 4th, 5th and 8ve. The 3rd, which we find so 'normal' and pleasant, they thought made a 'wicked' mixture and was certainly not suitable to be heard in church! During this time, rounds, canons, drones and ostinati (played on small drums and other instruments) became popular 'recipes'.

 (a) Listen to medieval songs, dances and pieces of church music. After each, discuss (i) what makes it sound old, (ii) whether any of the old instruments used remind you of modern ones, (iii) whether or not the music has a strong regular beat, (iv) whether any of the above 'recipes' was used, (v) why you like or dislike the music.

If possible, compare different performances of the same piece. Why are modern performers never certain they have got the music right?

In your notebook

(i) (Copy, filling in the missing words)
The Middle Ages or —— Period lasted for about —— centuries. It stretched from about the Battle of —— in the —— century to Joan —— —— in the —— century. Many of our —— songs were first sung by minstrels or —— at this time. As there was no exact musical code, the songs often changed as they were passed by word of mouth from ——. The favourite sound mixtures were the —— of a 4th, 5th and 8ve. Popular musical 'recipes' were the round or ——, —— and ——.

Assignments

(A) Use the above scale to draw lines representing the duration of (a) your life, (b) the life of the oldest person you know and (c) the Middle Ages. About how many of your grandfather's lives could fit end to end in the Middle Ages?

If a new generation is born every twenty-five years, your great-grandfather was born about a hundred years ago. About how many 'greats' are needed to describe your ancestor who fought at Agincourt? How many centuries ago was this?

(B) A number of important medieval people and events have been given/pictured. List these under a suitable heading, including:
(a) The important document signed by King John;
(b) The leader of the Peasant's Revolt;
(c) A king who was a singer;
(d) A terrible plague in the 14th century.
(C) Compare the way the rich and the poor lived. There are clues on these pages.
(D) Collect material associated with medieval music, instruments and life generally. Make use of record sleeves, books, pictures and visits to any local medieval buildings or exhibitions.

10 SOUNDS ANCIENT AND MODERN

Medieval intruments

A medieval tune: 'Song of the Ass'

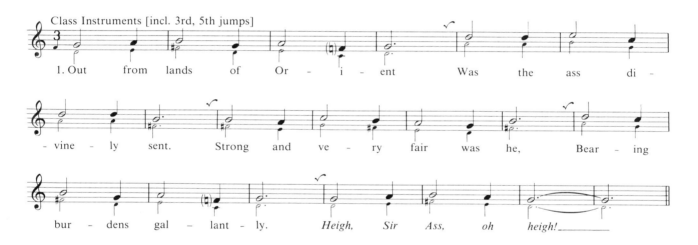

Class Instruments [incl. 3rd, 5th jumps]

1. Out from lands of Or – i – ent   Was the ass di –
– vine – ly sent.   Strong and ve – ry fair was he,   Bear – ing
bur – dens gal – lant – ly.   *Heigh, Sir Ass, oh heigh!*____

Things to do

1. Now add these accompaniments to the song:

(a) A second voice part a 4th below (small notes).

(b) Some pupils playing either or both parts on comb and paper.

(c) A 5th drone:

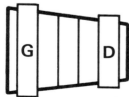

both notes being played on any class instruments (including melodicas). Low-pitched instruments just play G. All play every three beats.

(d) Ostinati as follows:

drum

tambourine

The pattern of an ostinato may have to be broken to make a good ending.

Why is it appropriate to play this music on the recorder and add a drone and ostinati? Does the song remind you of a particular hymn tune? If so, in what ways is it different?

(a) Hear different recordings of the 'Song of the Ass'.

(b) Listen to more medieval dances on record. Take turns at adding two ostinati to each piece, using a small drum and triangle/bell:

(i) Copy rhythms from the music.
(ii) Improvise your own short patterns.
You will be told the names of the instruments used in the recordings. Look at their pictures below and on record sleeves.

Recorders would be ideal for playing the above song. Although finally developed in the Middle Ages, the ones you can buy, like the other 'old' instruments heard in recordings, will be modern copies. The pictures below show some of the many instruments that were around in the medieval period. Although only one example of each is given, they were often made in different sizes to correspond with the various singing pitches. So descant, SOPRANO (treble),

Soprano or descant recorder

ALTO,

Alto or treble recorder

TENOR

Tenor recorder

and BASS

Bass recorder

can describe instruments as well as voices. This includes recorders and class intruments like the glockenspiel.

As life was much harder long ago, people got special pleasure from big feasts, glamorous clothes, strong contrasts and bright colours generally. The instruments they played also had well-contrasted sounds. Those with the loudest and brightest sound were used outdoors for processions and dancing and the quieter and more mellow instruments, like the recorder, were only used indoors. Here are other medieval instruments, and the names of any modern 'relatives':

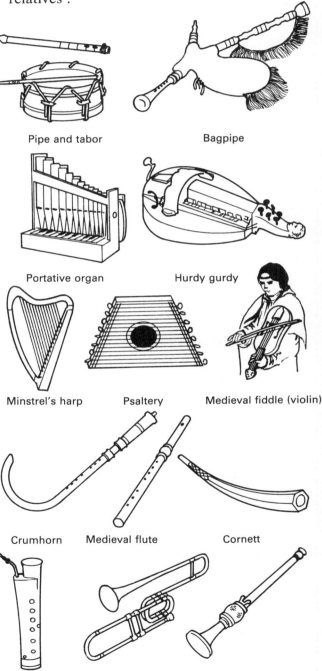

Pipe and tabor Bagpipe

Portative organ Hurdy gurdy

Minstrel's harp Psaltery Medieval fiddle (violin)

Crumhorn Medieval flute Cornett

Dulcian (bassoon) Sackbut (trombone) Shawm (oboe)

In your notebook

(i) (Copy, filling in the missing words)
Medieval instruments were divided into out-door and——types. Instruments like the——come in different sizes and match the singing pitch of ladies or boys (——, ——and——) and gentlemen (——and bass). Three medieval instruments I have heard are——, —— and——.

(c) Listen to a recording demonstrating medieval instruments. Try to remember the sound of each one. Are you ever reminded of modern instruments? Discuss (i) whether they are 'outdoor' or 'indoor' ones and (ii) which page 5 group each belongs to.

(d) Now hear more medieval instrumental and vocal music. Identify any instruments and listen for ostinati, drones and canons.

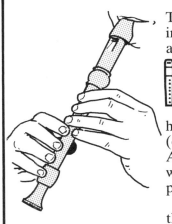

This is a good time to start playing the descant recorder, an old 'indoor' instrument that is now very popular again. Ignore these sections if you play already, or if no instruments are available.

indicates that the music is suitable for recorder players starting now. It will help your music reading if you also play this music on fixed-pitch instruments where the 'notes' can be seen.

As each finger 'belongs' to a particular hole, first make them all feel at home, as in the picture. Higher pitches are made by 'shortening' the tube (opening the holes); lower pitches by 'lengthening' it (closing the holes). Always keep each finger above its hole. Whenever you play, get in tune with each other (or with other instruments) by adjusting (twisting, not pulling) the length of your instrument.

Each note will be shown as a diagram. The finger numbers start from the thumb (1). Here is your first one:

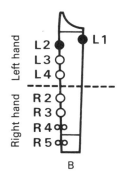

Cover the thumb hole (L1) and hole (L2). Place the right thumb underneath, opposite R3, and all other fingers above their holes. Place the mouthpiece just on the lower lip and close the upper lip snugly round it. Now whisper this rhythm in one breath, tonguing 'too':

Think of breathing gently rather than blowing. Hear (a) the pitch sharpen when you blow too hard; (b) the pitch flatten when you breathe too gently. Repeat with the second note.

Next, play the notes in succession—still in one breath:

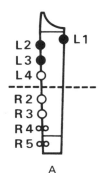

Now play the rhythm of 'Jingle Bells' and other simple songs on note A. Only breathe between the phrases. Repeat with note B. Finally, echo back short phrases using these notes. Some of the following rhythm acitivites could be played on the recorder as well.

● Covered hole
○ Open hole

Minims

An Irish folk-song: 'Gypsy Rover'

1. The gyp-sy ro-ver came o-ver the hill, Bound through the val-ley so sha-dy; He
CHORUS Ah - di - do, ah-di-do-da-day, Ah - di - do, ah-di-day - dee; He

whist-led and he sang till the green-woods rang, And he won the heart of a la — — —dy.
whist-led and he sang till the green-woods rang, And he won the heart of a la — — —dy.

Things to do

2. In three groups, play the letters given with the above song. Make each note two beats long. Then accompany the singing.

3. Here is the opening rhythm of 'Land of Hope and Glory' with the last two notes missing:

Now, in two groups, clap the rhythm against the regular beat. For how many beats does each missing note last?

This note ♩ lasts for two crotchet beats and is called a MINIM.

Here are four minims, showing how two crotchets and four quavers can fit neatly against each one:

Instead of saying 'grand' and 'father' to get the rhythm right, change to these more appropriate words:

'c r a w l'   'w a l k'   'run-ning'

In your notebook

(ii) Draw and label a minim, explaining how long it lasts. Now copy the given three lines of notes, again like an addition sum, to show how they fit against each other.

Things to do

4. Count the number of ♪, ♫, ♩ and 𝅗𝅥 printed in 'Gypsy Rover'.
5. Repeat Chapter 6, 20–22, using the above rhythm words.
6. Clap crotchet beats at a given tempo. Then, in two groups, and at the same tempo, clap minims against crotchets while also saying 'crawl' and 'walk'. Did you find yourself nodding the second beat half-way through each 'crawl'?

Now divide into three groups and similarly clap and say minims, crotchets and quavers. Look at the given illustration as you fit them together. At a signal, each group change to the note value below (or return to the first one).

Repeat, using contrasted pitched or unpitched instruments, and at different tempi.

7. First practise these rhythms by clapping and saying the rhythm words. Later, repeat each one a given number of times:

Now in two or more groups, combine any of them played four times (i) just saying the words, (ii) clapping and saying the words and (iii) playing on contrasted unpitched instruments as indicated. Four players accompany 'Gypsy Rover' with ostinati as in (iii).

8. Similarly treat these rhythms as (i), (ii) and (iii) above:

Now, in four groups using contrasted unpitched instruments, combine with the rhythms

of 1(d). Finally, all accompany 'The Song of the Ass' as it is played on the piano or a record.

9. In two or more groups, perform rounds using the rhythms from 7 in succession and performing methods (i), (ii) or (iii). At first, Delay each start by one line. Later, experiment with shorter delays.

10. Repeat 9 with each group playing one pitch on class instruments or recorder (A or B). Mix either DFAB or FGAC.

11. Each compose your own eight-beat rhythm as in 7, using similar note values. Combine rhythms as above.

12. Write down similar short rhythms played to you.

13. Practise and combine these rhythms as above, obeying the *f* and *p* instructions (also damp if necessary):

(a) 𝅗𝅥 𝅘𝅥 𝅘𝅥 𝅘𝅥 𝅗𝅥 𝅗𝅥 𝅘𝅥 𝅘𝅥𝅘𝅥 𝅘𝅥 𝅘𝅥 𝅗𝅥 𝅗𝅥
   f   *p*   *f*

(b) 𝅗𝅥 𝅗𝅥 𝅘𝅥 𝄽 𝅘𝅥 𝄽 𝅘𝅥 𝅗𝅥   𝅗𝅥 𝅘𝅥 𝅘𝅥𝅘𝅥 𝅘𝅥 𝄽 𝅘𝅥
   f   *p*   *f*

14. Turn to 'Sumer is icumen in' on page 28. The second part should preferably be sung at a lower 8ve by tenors/basses. Perform this way if broken voices are available, adding the drone and ostinati as before.

(e) Compare the sound of the different recorders as you listen to solos on descant, treble, etc. instruments. Which do you prefer?

(f) Listen to music written for a group of different-sized recorders. As some modern composers are writing for the recorder again, you may hear both old and new music in (e) and (f).

Assignment

(A) Conduct a voice survey among all the adults you know. List the numbers of sopranos, altos, tenors and basses. From these compile class totals.

11 THE SOUND OF MUSIC

Tonic solfa

 (a) Listen to a recording of the following song and then sing it yourselves (the words are below):

From *The Sound of Music*: 'Doh Ray Me'

I hope you realise that your singing voice is a musical instrument. In fact, during the Middle Ages, and much of the time since, many composers have written their best music for voices.

The idea of arranging the different pitches in a row, called a SCALE, is a very old one. So is the idea of giving each pitch a letter name or a singing name. In the song you heard the singing names often used today. There is a reason why they are rather odd. At about the time of William the Conqueror, an Italian monk called Guido d'Arezzo noticed that the lines of a Latin hymn started one note higher each time. As it was familiar to his pupils, he thought it would be a good idea to use the first syllable of each line as the singing names of his scale. Provided they remembered how each line began, the pupils had a useful code for writing and reading pitch.

Although the syllables have changed since then, you can see that today's system, called (TONIC) SOLFA, is very similar—and that the above song is not such a new idea!

	DOH′
	that will bring us back to
	TE, a drink with jam and bread
LA-bii reatum	LAH, a note to follow soh
SOL-ve polluti	SOH, a needle pulling thread
FA-muli tuorum	FAH, a long long way to run
MI-ragestorum	ME, a name I call myself
RE-sonare fibris	RAY, a drop of golden sun
UT quant lavis	DOH, a deer, a female deer

These singing names are often shortened to single letters. The pattern repeats both higher and lower—just like the letter names. Notes with the same 'family' sound again have the same name, and, of course, are an octave apart. Intervals are still measured in the same way, as the 'Interval Ruler' shows. (The notes of higher and lower 8ves are shown by using upper and lower dashes.)

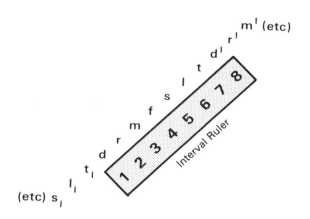

In your notebook

(Copy, completing the words)
(i) The different p——can be arranged in a row called a sc——. They can have letter names or singing names called s——. The repeating pattern of singing names is doh,——, ——, ——, ——, ——, ——, and then ——again.

Things to do

1. Listen to a phrase starting from doh. It will either step up or down one note at a time or repeat the same pitch. 'Shadow' the phrase with a finger on the above scale/ruler. On which note does each phrase end?
2. The following song openings also only step or repeat pitches:

    m
(a) 'My old man's a dustman, he wears a dustman's hat'
    m
(b) 'One man went to mow, went to mow a meadow'
    m
(c) 'Rule Britannia, Britannia rules the waves'

    m
(d) 'The first Nowell the angel did say, was to certain poor shepherds in fields'
    s
(e) 'The hills are alive with the sound of music'
    f
(f) 'Close your eyes, and I'll kiss you' ('All My Loving'—Beatles)

First learn any unfamiliar ones, and then sing each one while moving a hand up or down, with the pitch. Finally, from the given starting note, 'finger' each tune up and down the above solfa scale as you 'sing' it in your head. Identify each last note.

3. Echo back short phrases sung to you in solfa. The notes will only step or repeat.
4. Practise singing from d up to d' and back again. Later, go a little way into the next octave up or down.
5. With a s, to m' scale on the board as shown and starting from doh, sing solfa up and down as indicated by a pointer.
6. Sing each of these rows of stepping notes to solfa:

        d r m f s l t d'
        d r m f

Now, in two groups, sing them together, the second group delaying its start as shown. Sing at a steady tempo and hold the last notes on together. What interval row did you sing? What sort of music does it remind you of? Treat the following in the same way. What interval row do these make?

        d r m f s l s f m
        d r m f m r d

7. Clap these rhythms, first, 'singing' the song openings in your head, and then saying the rhythm words 'walk', crawl 'or' running':

'Three blind mice,   three blind mice'
(a) d   t,   d   r   r   d
(b) d   r   d   d   r   m
(c) d   r   m   f   s   s
(d) d   t,   l,   l,   t,   d

'Hap-py birth-day to   you,   hap-py birth-day to you'
(e) d d r   r   d   r   d d r   d   r   d
(f) d d d   r   m   r   m f s   s   f   m
(g) d' d' d' t   l   s   s l t   l   l   s
(h) d t, l, t,   d   t,   d d t, l, t, d

39

Now sing each stepping solfa phrase in the given rhythm. Finally, in groups, sing two or more from any set simultaneously.

8. Join the phrases of each of the above sets into complete tunes and sing in succession. Later, in four groups, sing each set as a round, delaying each entry by one line. For a change, sometimes stop the round when the first group reaches the end.

Moving doh

So far in your solfa singing, the pitch of doh has been the same. This need not have been so. The singing names, unlike the fixed letter code, may start at any pitch: e.g.

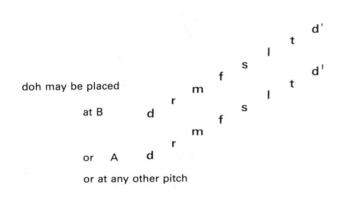

This means that when you change doh in the following activities, the other notes of the scale will have to change pitch with it:

Things to do

9. Repeat some activities from 1 to 8, with doh at different pitches. Also, try singing 'la' to all the notes, instead of solfa.

10. Below are some solfa scales to be sung in various rhythms. Some ascend, some descend from doh', while others go both ways. Clap each one, saying the rhythm words aloud or in your head before singing it.

Now, in groups, combine the bracketed rhythms (i) saying the rhythm words, (ii) clapping and saying the words and (iii) just clapping. Finally, combine the groups of scales sung to solfa. If you change doh, 'lay the trail' first by singing a practice scale from doh to doh'.

Stave lines and spaces

You should already have discovered that it is not always easy to sing from a pitch code that keeps level. Something that goes up and down like the bosun's pipe code on page 17 would be far more helpful to the eye. In 11 below, you will find that it is even harder to play letters with a level code. Although:

We prefer our keyboards horizontal

DOWN ← → UP

UP

DOWN

and not vertical!

Things to do

11. As many pupils as possible take (or share) a class instrument or piano covering one 8ve from C to C. Have races playing the following notes as quickly as possible: (A) CDEFGABC, (b) CBAGFEDC, (c) CABBAGE, (d) FDAGCBE. What makes each series get gradually harder?

Right at the beginning of the Middle Ages composers realised that an up and down help was necessary. Performers need warning of where a tune is going. They started off by having a single horizontal line and putting their funny code above and below it. This was not very exact, so they improved matters by having two coloured lines instead (find these two codes on page 31). Later, further lines were added, and it has settled for the past four hundred years into the familiar five-line ladder. A ladder like

this that shows the pitch of notes is called a STAVE or STAFF:

On a stave, the different pitches can be shown exactly by alternately using both

LINES ── and SPACES ──

Unlike on this kind of ladder!

As in the Middle Ages, we will first use just one stave line. If we use it for letters it is a fixed code, with B always on the line:

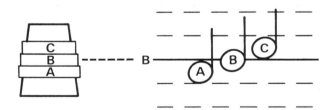

When you play class instruments, any 8ve may be played. If a stave is used for solfa, doh may be placed on any line or space. A ■ shows the changing positions of doh:

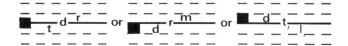

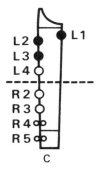

Here is your next recorder note. The fingerings for the first two notes are given again underneath. These three fit on the single line stave as shown on the previous page.

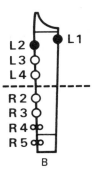

When you have practised going from each note to the others, play the pieces indicated below. Play each phrase in one breath. Later, lines of more than one phrase will have the breathing places marked with a ⌄ . Long phrases need a quick, deep gulp, with the air being breathed out very sparingly.

It will help if you imagine your lungs as a blown-up balloon. Have you ever squirted air out of a balloon very gradually — making nasty squeaking noises! With care, you can make one 'blowing' last a long time. Playing recorder phrases is rather like that. Letting the air out very gradually from your lung 'balloon' will enable you to play long phrases in just one breath.

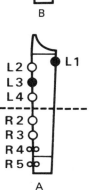

Things to do

12. Play the following phrases on chime bars, glockenspiel, metallophone or piano, sharing the same instrument at different octaves when possible. (a) to (e) are in the rhythm of 'Three Blind Mice' and (f) to (j) are in the rhythm of 'Happy Birthday to you' (see 7). The pitches required for each one are given on the left:

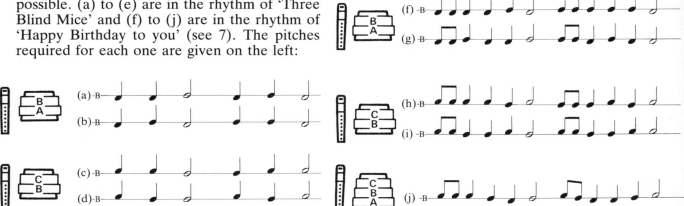

13. Similarly play the following. Clap each rhythm first:

Now play (a) and (b) in succession as an accompaniment to 'Three Blind Mice'. Similarly, play (c) and (d) with 'Jingle Bells'.

14. Listen to phrases from 12 and 13 played with
(a) a mistake in the rhythm, (b) a mistake in the pitch. Write what was played, or say what was wrong.

15. The following phrases each have one note missing at ×. Copy them down, and insert the missing pitch as each is played with its gap filled. Add a 𝅗𝅥 in (a) to (d), and a 𝅗𝅥 or 𝅘𝅥 in (e) to (h):

16. Write down the solfa names of these notes. Use the s₁ to m' scale on page 39 to help you work out the line/space journey from each doh:

(a) (b) (c) (d)   (e) (f) (g) (h)   (i) (j) (k) (l)

17. Now use the stave as a singing code. Sing the following:

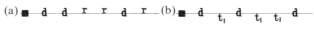

Next, write them out properly as in 18 below, repeating the 'Three Blind Mice' rhythm. Again sing to solfa, but now in the correct rhythm.

18. Each phrase in 12 and 13 can be turned into a singing code. Make each first note doh. Here are 12(a) and 13(a) done for you:

Sing these phrases to solfa. Sing others when you have rewritten them.

19. First clap the rhythm, and then sing the following:

Now sing both in immediate succession. Finally, one group repeat this as an accompaniment to the other group singing the 'Doh, Ray, Me' song at the same tempo. Later, play on class instruments or recorder.

20. Repeat 18 and 19, singing 'lah' instead of solfa.

21. Discuss the following:
(a) Why solfa is more difficult to read when printed level, and not on a stave;
(b) Where in Britain solfa reading is still popular;
(c) Why letter names, but not solfa, can be permanently marked on, for example, a piano or chime bar.

12 THE SOUND OF WORDS

Word rhythms

Things to do

1. Use suitable class instruments to accompany the song, playing (a) either or both the letters written above the words, (b) the one-line stave part.
2. Find the song's highest and lowest notes.

How many times does each occur? What are their solfa names if the song begins on doh? The words and rhythms match each other exactly. List the *single* words the composer fits to each (a) ♩ , (b) ♩ and (c) ♫

'Salt, Mustard, Vinegar'

So, there are many words that fit each note value. The 'walk', 'crawl' and 'running' system seems a good one as the meanings as well as the sounds are so appropriate. However, it can be fun to invent other systems for these three notes:

	♩	♩ (half note)	♫
	walk	crawl	run-ning
Football teams	Hull	Leeds	Burn-ley
Girls' names	Anne	Joan	Ju-lie
Drinks	coke	beer	cof-fee

Words with more than one syllable need a note for each one. In music, the different syllables should always be separated by hyphens, with the notes written exactly above each one.

Things to do

3. Invent further systems for ♩ , 𝅗𝅥 and ♫ , using (a) the above categories and (b) food, games, etc.

Use your systems in previous activities.

4. First practise each rhythm in succession, saying the given words. Later, use other systems:

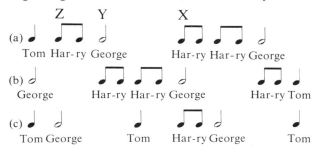

(a) Tom Har-ry George Har-ry Har-ry George

(b) George Har-ry Har-ry George Har-ry Tom

(c) Tom George Tom Har-ry George Tom

Then combine (i) starting together and (ii) as a round, with a one-line delay at first, and later coming in at X, Y or Z.

5. Compose three rhythms, each totalling 16 ♩ beat's worth. Again use only ♩ , 𝅗𝅥 and ♫ , setting out as in 4 so that longer notes have more space. Next, choose one to perform simultaneously with the rest of the class. Say words or use unpitched instruments.

Longer words and all phrases usually need a mixture of different note values:

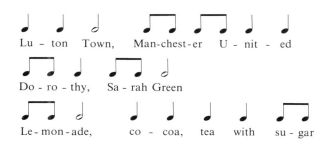

Lu – ton Town, Man-chest-er U – nit – ed

Do – ro – thy, Sa – rah Green

Le – mon-ade, co – coa, tea with su – gar

Longer groups of words can also be joined:

West Ham U – ni – ted and Ply-mouth Arg – yle

Things to do

6. Clap and say the above phrase four times. Now, in four groups, perform as a round, each part coming in (i) at X, (ii) at Y.
Repeat, clapping only.

7. Match words to rhythms, and then write both out as above:
(a) Mus-ic les-sons are far too long
(b) Our team will win the cup
(c) North A-mer-i-can towns are bu-sy
(d) Boys be-have much bet-ter than girls

8. First write out the following, separating each syllable with a hyphen. Add ♩ , 𝅗𝅥 and ♫ above the remaining syllables.

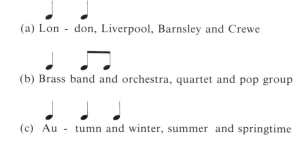

(a) Lon – don, Liverpool, Barnsley and Crewe

(b) Brass band and orchestra, quartet and pop group

(c) Au – tumn and winter, summer and springtime

(d) Tea, ci-der, vinegar, champagne

Perform and compare your answers. You will see that it is usually possible to do them different ways.

When composers set words to music, they sometimes write more than one note to a syllable. When this happens they use a SLUR ⌣ to indicate the notes that are sung to that syllable (and a dash after the syllable):

'Land of hope – and glo – ry'

Things to do

9. Find the slur in 'Gypsy Rover' (page 36). Now find slurs in any song or hymn books you have.

10. Write out the following song openings, separating each syllable as shown. Then, sing each aloud or in your head while clapping with the beat. Notice where a second beat 'pumps' through a minim. Now write the correct note value(s) above each syllable. Use a slur when necessary. Each one has been started for you.

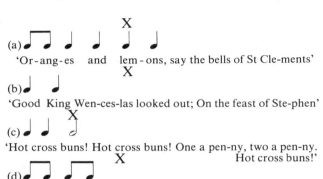

(a) 'Or–ang–es and lem–ons, say the bells of St Cle–ments'

(b) 'Good King Wen–ces–las looked out; On the feast of Ste–phen'

(c) 'Hot cross buns! Hot cross buns! One a pen–ny, two a pen–ny. Hot cross buns!'

(d) 'Bob–by Shaf–toe's gone to sea, sil–ver buck–les on his knee'

11. Clap and say each as a two-part canon from X. Now copy and complete the following, which shows how the first canon fits together.

Finally, write out the other three canons similarly.

12. Repeat Chapter 11, 2. Now write out the words with the syllables separated and add the solfa letters above each one. You will need to use some slurs: e.g.

(d) The First Now – ell,

13. Sing chapter 11, 2(f) again and then add the correct note values above the solfa.

14. Compose solfa phrases using the rhythms of 10 written on the board. Place ▪ as below and begin and end each phrase on doh. Do not jump over any notes. Here is a possible start for (a):

All sing selected tunes written on the board. Later, play them on class instruments/recorders.

15. Write down its letter as any of the following are played. Identify using the 'up, down, same' principle:

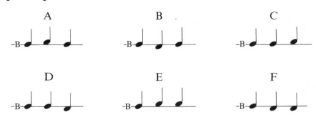

Later, identify words as several are played in quite close succession.

16. Write down a phrase played slowly in the rhythm shown:

It will start at C and only repeat or step up or down as in 16.

Accents and time

Things to do

17. In two groups, clap a regular beat against each of the phrases from 10, spoken or sung. Notice which syllables seem to want to be louder. Now exaggerate the louder syllables and beats. Finally, just for fun, make the wrong syllables louder. Discuss whether the beats with strong syllables make any kinds of patterns.

So, the beat is not the only regular thing about most music. The stronger beats or ACCENTS (>) also come round regularly. Any pattern of stronger and weaker boats is called the music's TIME or METRE.

In DUPLE TIME the pattern is

| | strong | weak | strong | weak | |
| | > | | > | | etc. |

and can be counted: 1 2 1 2

as in: 'Jin-gle bells, jin-gle bells'

In QUADRUPLE TIME the pattern is

	strong	weak	weak	weak	strong	
	>				>	etc.
and can be counted:	1	2	3	4	1	
as in:	'land	of	hope	and	glo-ry'	

Duple and quadruple times are very similar. They both come from walking and marching movements.

In TRIPLE TIME the pattern is

	strong	weak	weak	strong	weak	weak	
and can	>			>			etc.
be counted:	1	2	3	1	2	3	
as in:	'God	save	our	Grac -	ious	Queen'	

This comes from the very different, flowing movements of older dances.

In your notebook

(i) (Copy, unjumbling the words)
Most music has a regular strong beat or *cantec*. This comes every two beats in *pudel* time, every *heter* beats in triple time and every four beats in *larqued up* time.

 (a) Listen to (i) pieces played on the piano and (ii) instrumental recordings. Work out the time of each by counting the beats, as in the above patterns. Make each accent beat 1. Repeat, with everybody clapping and counting the time.

So, even music without words is usually in duple, triple or quadruple time.

Things to do

18. Clap the rhythms of both 10 above and Chapter 11, 2, accenting correctly. Now write down the time of each.
19. Write an accent above the strong syllables of Chapter 11, 2. Here is the first one done for you:

>   >   >   >

'My old man's a dust-man, he wears a dust-man's hat'

Compare the beginnings of the first three songs with the second three.

You have discovered that words and word phrases do not always begin with a strong syllable. Very many words, phrases and poems begin with a weak syllable. This means that many songs must begin with a weak beat to match the words. Even instrumental music without words often begins with a weak beat. It is important to accent music properly.

 (b) Listen to piano and recorded instrumental music. After you have worked out the time of each piece, hear the beginning again. Does it begin on a strong or a weak beat?

Things to do

20. Listen to the opening phrases of piano pieces or songs played on the piano, each correctly beginning with a weak beat. Now hear the effect as the opening weak beat is made strong.
21. Listen to a ticking clock or metronome. Say 'tick tock' or 'one two' to yourself as you listen. At a signal, all say the words. Were you all in step?

We like regular accents so much that, when we hear beats that are all equally loud, we imagine that some of them are louder. Again listen as above, saying 'tick tock' to yourself. Change step by saying two 'ticks' in a row.
22. Now see how difficult it is to speak, clap, hit an instrument and even walk at a regular speed without making regular stronger movements or sounds as well.
23. March or mark time to a recording of a military march. Try doing the same to a waltz.
24. Combine rhythms from 10. Which times mix well? Now mix triple and quadruple time counting. Do the (exaggerated) accents ever coincide?
25. Discuss the following:
(a) Why the way you speak could affect a word rhythm code;
(b) Why duple time comes from walking movements;
(c) Whether three beats always means three notes;
(d) Why the rhythm might make you confuse the time.
26. Take or share a class pitched instrument, or assemble chime bars to make one of these words: FEED, DEAF, FADE, AGED, FAGGED.

Improvise an ostinato against a counted duple, triple or quadruple background. Play the letters in any interesting rhythm (a) once in order, (b) in any order (repeating letters). Repeat ostinati as instructed and combine in groups.

13   TIME AND A HALF

Dotted notes

Things to do

1. In two groups, clap this rhythm against a regular crotchet beat. There is a note missing at ×:

'The hills are a-live   with the sound of   mu - sic'

(a) What is its time?
(b) Does it begin on beat 1?
(c) How long is the missing note?

Sausages on sticks' show that the

code doubles each time. The next note in the system will therefore have a duration of four crotchets. But we want a note lasting for three crotchet beats! What can we do?

We can join or TIE two notes together:

Or, we can make any note half as long again by putting a DOT after it. For example:

In an imaginary dotted world we would have

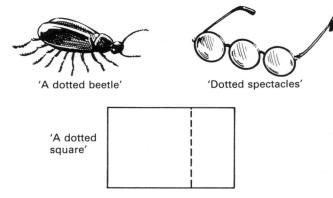

'A dotted beetle'   'Dotted spectacles'

'A dotted square'

In your notebook

(Copy, completing the words)
(i) A t —— joins two or more notes together into one long note. It is a curved line just like a sl——.
(ii) A d —— placed after any note makes that note half as long again.

Things to do

2. In a 'dotty' world what would be the value of: a dotted pound coin, a dotted 5p piece, a dotted centimetre, a dotted dozen, a dotted centipede and dotted twins?
3. Copy the words and rhythm from 1, adding the missing dotted minim. Now work out the rhythm of 'O Little town of Beth-le-hem how still we see thee lie' and set out similarly.

It is not so easy to use the 'running', 'walk', 'crawl' system with really long notes. We certainly never hold on syllables for three beats in normal speech. Musicians therefore usually count the beats to keep in time. For example:

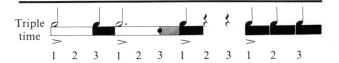

Triple time

1 2 3   1 2 3   1 2 3   1 2 3

Players need to be careful with long notes. As each number only marks the *beginning* of a beat, you can see that a two-beat note must normally last up to the *third* count. Similarly, a three-beat note should not stop sounding until the *fourth* count arrives. The same thing applies to the silences of rests.

Half-beat notes can be placed midway between counts by saying 'and' (&):

This also shows you how the counting system works when music begins on a weaker beat.

Always remember, long notes and rests must be kept in time by feeling the beats 'pumping' steadily through them. It helps to make a movement of some kind. For example, players can nod their head on each beat during long notes and rests. You will be strongly tempted to play in rests on strong beats! When clapping, keep your hands together during long notes and apart during rests. In both cases 'pump' your hands or nod your head with each beat.

Things to do

4. Play a single 𝅗𝅥 and 𝅗𝅥. on a fading pitched or unpitched instrument. Damp on the correct beat. Change the beat tempo.

5. Repeat each of the following, counting as you clap:

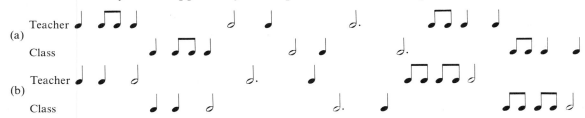

Now play on instruments, damping when necessary. Later, combine the patterns.

6. Clap and count the two 'sausage' rhythms given, accenting each beat 1. Be careful not to accent the first note of the second rhythm.

7. Echo these rhythms clapped to you. Repeat at different tempi:

Later, play on suitable instruments.

8. First, clap and count each of the following:

Now play on instruments. Make sure the only sound during rests is your counting.

Next, clap or play rhythms (a) and (b) four times like an ostinato. Then, using contrasted instruments, combine these ostinati. Repeat, using rhythms (c) and (d).

Finally, perform rhythms (a) and (b) in succession, and then as a round with a delay of one line. Treat rhythms (c) and (d) similarly.

When going well, stop counting aloud in all the above.

9. Write down a rhythm played while 1 2 3 4 is counted. It will contain only ♩ , ♫ , ♩ or ♩.

10. Write out rhythm 8(a) as 'sausages on sticks'.

Set out with the normal notes and counts as on page 49.

Discuss the advantages and disadvantages of the 'sausages' system.

A three-line stave

It is time we enlarged our stave to three lines. A single stave line hardly holds many notes! Remember, although the position of doh may move:

the letters are always fixed:

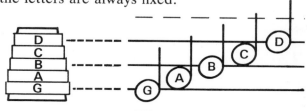

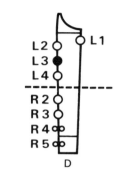

The next two recorder notes go above and below the ones you already know. Their position on the stave is shown. D requires the thumbhole (L1) to be uncovered.

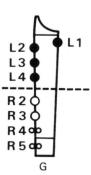

When you have practised the scale from G to D and back again, you will be ready to play the first piece below.

Before playing any piece on class intruments, first move your beater(s) over the notes required. This will enable you to judge the distances while looking at the music as you play.

Remember, instruments come in different sizes.

Things to do

11. Here is rhythm 8(a) made into a tune using the fixed letter code. Play it on any suitable class or other pitched instrument. As the tune is just a scale, practise going up and down the required notes first.

Then clap the rhythm and finally play the tune properly. Nod the beats during long notes:

12. Here is the same rhythm made into another tune, but using the solfa singing code instead. This time, prepare the singing 'trail' before performing properly:

Later (a) play this tune on pitched instruments and (b) sing tune 11, making the first note (bottom line) doh.

13. Play these two-note stepping tunes. First clap the rhythm:

Now, in two groups, play them together. Finally, some pupils play them as an accompaniment to 'Clementine'. Also try singing 'la' as you play.

14. Similarly perform these three-note stepping tunes. They can be used as an accompaniment to 'Ten Green Bottles':

15. Draw a three-line stave. Turn rhythm 8(a) into another stepping or repeating note tune, this time starting and ending on A or C. Why will you need to plan your tune in rough first? Play the tunes voted the best.

Jumping a 3rd

Up to now we have only thought of intervals being played as a mixture:

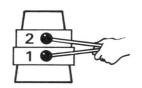

It is the same interval, and it is also measured the same, when the two notes are played in succession in a tune:

Your music reading so far has been made easier by giving you tunes that only repeat the same note or go up and down a note at a time. You are less likely to trip up when just stepping next door—an interval of a

2nd e.g.

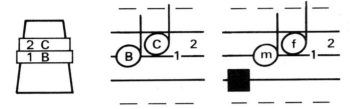

You might have a little more trouble now. The tunes are going to include a jump of two steps at once to the next-door-but-one note—an interval of a

3rd e.g.

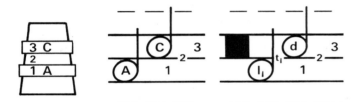

We say that notes are either in a space

or on a line

Do not confuse music with ordinary writing where 'on a line' means this:

bad

Next-door notes (2nds) are easily recognised. They go from a space to the next line

or from a line to the next space

up or down.

3rds are also easy to see. They go neatly from any line to the next one

(jumping over a space) or similarly from space to space

(jumping over a line). Notice how intervals are always measured upwards. Remember, notes on next-door lines or spaces are not next-door!

When reading singing music it is often helpful to 'lay the trail' first. This means singing over the notes used in the tune. Now that your solfa tunes are going to include jumps it will be particularly helpful to do this.

The 'trail' is laid by first singing the given notes both up and down. Then repeat, but singing any bracketed notes in your head. Finally, miss them out altogether and sing the 'trail' straight up and down.

Imagining missing notes in your head will always help you across intervals and enable you to find the first note if it is not doh. Before reading both singing and playing music it also often helps to first clap the rhythm. Use either the counting system or rhythm words. Music first sung to solfa can also be repeated and sung to 'la' or some other syllable.

Things to do

16. (dr)m(f)s [introducing 3rd jump: m-s]

17. (dr)m(f)sl [incl. 3rd jump]

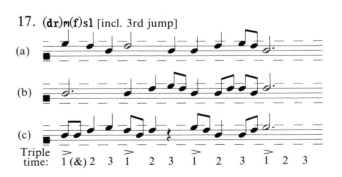

18. In three groups, combine the phrases of 16. Enjoy holding on the mixture at the end. Then sing in succession as a canon with a one-line delay. Repeat with 17.

19. When you have learnt the following, sing it as an accompaniment to 'One Man Went to Mow' or 'My Old Man's a Dustman'. Either:
(a) All accompany the song played on the piano;
(b) One group accompany another group singing the song:

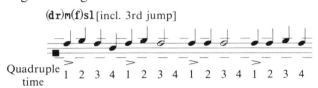

(d r)m(f)sl [incl. 3rd jump]

Quadruple time   1 2 3 4   1 2 3 4   1 2 3 4   1 2 3 4

20. Copy these openings which include intervals of a 3rd. Complete the solfa above each syllable:

m
(a) 'Three Blind Mice, Three Blind Mice'
d
(b) 'God Save our Grac-ious Queen'

You ought to be able to sing (and recognise) the interval of a 3rd. The cuckoo manages very well:

And so do many warning sirens and door bells!

Things to do

21. Recognise whether two notes sung in succession up or down are a 2nd or 3rd apart. Let the cuckoo help you!
22. The following phrases each have two notes missing at ×.
    Copy them and insert the missing notes as

each is sung to 'la' with the gap filled in various ways. The notes used will be chosen from (a) me, soh (b) me, soh, lah:

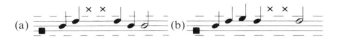

(a)   (b)

23. Now take instruments to play this tune:

(a)

Quadruple time   1 2 3 4   1 2 3 4   1 2 3 4   1 2 3 4

and then this one, containing both 3rds and single steps (2nds):

(b)

Quadruple time   1 2 3 4   1 2 3 4   1 2 3 4   1 2 3 4

24. In two groups, play the above tunes together. Then take turns at playing them both as an accompaniment to the songs of 19.
    Later, try singing the songs as you play. Finally, combine with some singing as in 19(b).
25. Compose and play a tune similar to 23(b). Use the same rhythm, 2nds and 3rds only, and begin and end on A or C.
26. Treat the following as in Chapter 12, 15:

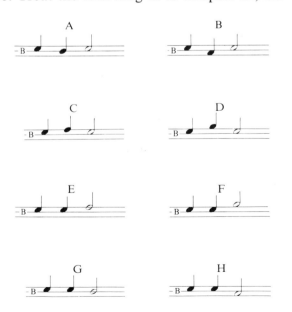

27. Turn to page 60. Identify all the intervals in the two tunes that are not 2nds or 3rds.

WARS OF THE ROSES	Henry VIII	Elizabeth I
	Copernicus	ARMADA
	Vasco da Gama	Raleigh
	Magellan	Drake
Caxton		Shakespeare
Columbus	Thomas More	
	Luther	
	REFORMATION	
	Michelangelo	
	Leonardo da Vinci	

14   THE RENAISSANCE

The fifteenth and especially the sixteenth centuries were great periods of discovery for Western Europe. Scholars started to explore the past and particularly began to admire the ancient civilisations of Greece and Rome. They even started to revive their building styles:

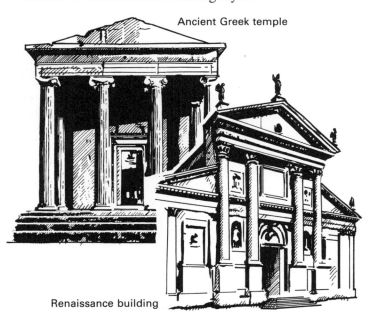

Ancient Greek temple

Renaissance building

Sailors discovered new lands, and scientists started making people think in more modern ways:

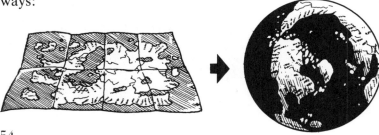

This great period was called the RENAIS-SANCE or re-birth. It was like 'turning over a new leaf', and new fashions began to appear in many things.

Musicians began writing music more like what we are used to today and the invention of music printing encouraged much musical performance. If you go to one of our cathedrals you will often hear music by sixteenth-century composers like Palestrina (Italy) and our own Thomas Tallis, William Byrd and Orlando Gibbons. Their church music does not have a very strong beat and seems to flow on like a stream without stops or phrases. Much of it is like an impolite conversation where different voices keep butting in—rather similar to a canon or round:

When the words sung were in Latin the pieces were called MASSES or MOTETS. Some of our composers, however, wrote ANTHEMS using English words. They were influenced by the REFORMATION, which tried to make the services and the music easier for ordinary people to understand.

MADRIGALS were also written in the Elizabethan period. The musical conversation in these was usually more lively as the words were secular poems. If you had belonged to a rich family you would have been expected to read music well and sing madrigals. This is what the English composer Thomas Morley wrote in 1597:

'But supper being ended, and Musicke bookes, according to the custome being brought to the table: the mistresse of the house presented mee with a part, earnestly requesting me to sing. But when after manie excuses, I protested unfainedly that I could not: everie one began to wonder. Yea, some whispered to others, demaunding how I was brought up.'

Printed music was looking much more like the familiar code, as you can see in the following madrigal. Why do you think it was arranged in such an odd way?

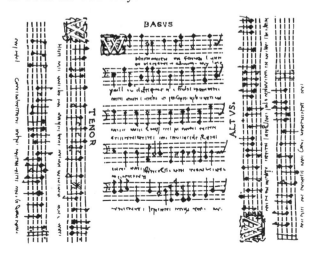

Henry VIII and Elizabeth I

There were still no orchestras or concerts at this time, and many of the older instruments remained in use. In the Elizabethan period, wealthy households often had their own sets of instruments such as the recorders.

Henry VIII was a good musician and possessed many instruments. He also fancied himself as a composer, even though he may have stolen other people's tunes as readily as he stole their wives!

The sixteenth century also had its popular songs which both rich and poor enjoyed. 'Greensleeves' was one of them, and so was 'Three Blind Mice', which was printed in a collection of rounds. It was a great time for dancing. Two particular favourites were the slow duple-time PAVANE and the fast-triple time GALLIARD.

(a) Listen to English madrigals. Notice how complicated it is when the singers keep butting in.
(b) Hear pavanes and galliards. Identify each from its time. Try to match the instrument(s) used with those shown on page 34.

In your notebook

(i) Write a paragraph on (a) madrigals and (b) Elizabethan dances.

Assignments

(A) List all the people in the chart on page 54. Add their nationality and what they were famous for.
(B) Find out about or visit any local buildings of this period. How do they compare with famous examples such as 'Hampton Court'?
(C) Write a paragraph explaining why the second half of the sixteenth century was a great time for Britain.

15   TONE AND A HALF

Tones and semitones

So far you have only read intervals 'longways' as part of a melody, e.g.

This is what these same intervals look like when written to be played together by one player:

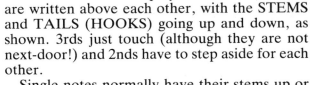

Notes intended to be played at the same time are written above each other, with the STEMS and TAILS (HOOKS) going up and down, as shown. 3rds just touch (although they are not next-door!) and 2nds have to step aside for each other.

Single notes normally have their stems up or down depending on which side of the middle line they are:

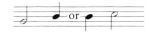

The fashion for preferring the mixtures of a 4th and 5th ended with the Middle Ages. From the Renaissance right down to our own century, the favourite mixture has been the 3rd—the 'next-door-but-one' interval.

Things to do

1. Use two beaters to play these intervals of a 3rd and 2nd. Later combine the parts. As only stepping movements are needed, you can look at the music and play by 'feel'.

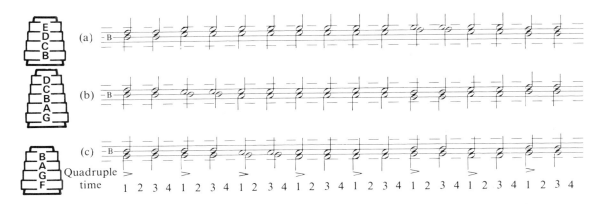

2. All practise the following alternate hand movements based on

Either use real instruments or pretend to play on your table. Keep at the same tempo. Which music-writing rules are broken in order for you to tell which hand to use?

3. Now play the intervals of 1, each broken up to make a 'zig-zag' tune of shorter notes as above. If necessary, first practise each interval change separately:

4. Play any or all of the phrases of 1 and 3 together.
5. Recognise 3rds and 2nds played as mixtures on the piano.
6. Hear these 2nds played on the piano:

B C D E F G A
A B C D E F G

Although they all share the harsh 'family flavour', which ones are the most clashing? Look at the keyboard and discuss why this is so.

Taking the piano lid off answers the question:

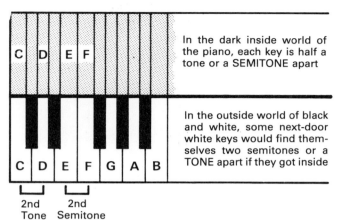

In the dark inside world of the piano, each key is half a tone or a SEMITONE apart

In the outside world of black and white, some next-door white keys would find themselves two semitones or a TONE apart if they got inside

Tones and semitones are both 2nds. They do not look different on a stave

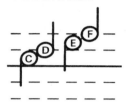

However, 2nds (especially when they are semitones) sound harsh when played together—but smooth and easy to sing, when stepping as a tune

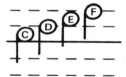

Yet, there is a place even for harsh mixtures in music. Did you notice how pleasant the 2nds sounded in Activities 1 and 3?

Instruments like the piano, containing all the semitones, are called CHROMATIC INSTRU-MENTS. Some class instruments are also chromatic:

Many, however, only have the 'white' keys. These are DIATONIC INSTRUMENTS:

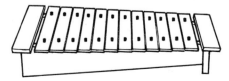

58

The disadvantage of these is that there are no 'landmarks' for finding notes (keys) quickly.

The chromatic instrument pattern does not have to be black and white. Any class instruments in your room may well have other colours. Many Renaissance and later keyboard instruments either have the colours reversed, or have different-coloured keys altogether. So it is really wrong to talk about 'black' and 'white' notes—although most people do! Certainly, very few people can identify them by their sound—can you?

Just think: if the keyboard was like this:

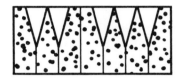

(and it could have been) we would be talking about 'pointed' and 'spotted' notes instead!

Things to do

7. See if you can recognise whether a piano note played is 'black' or 'white'.
8. Recognise tones and semitones (a) played as a mixture and (b) played in succession up or down.

In your notebook

(i) (Copy, completing the words)
Inside the piano all the 'notes' are a sem—— apart. However, because some of the outside keys are short bl——ones, not all the wh—— keys are a sem——apart. Some are two sem—— or a t——apart. The semitones are E to F and— to—. The tones are C to D, D to—, —to—, —to—and—to—.

Instruments having all the semitones, such as the p—— and o——, are called chr——.

Elizabethan music

Although the piano had not yet been invented, several instruments with keyboards were used in the Renaissance. The organ was getting larger and more complicated and the following instruments were particularly popular. You may have seen original Renaissance examples in museums or stately homes.

They are often beautifully decorated:

The HARPSICHORD family, which includes the smaller SPINET and VIRGINALS, have strings which are plucked by quills

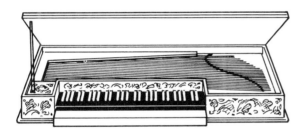

The very quiet CLAVICHORD has pieces of metal (tangents) that press on to the ends of the strings

Even Queen Elizabeth I liked playing the virginals. It was said by a foreign ambassador:

'The Queen plaied quite well upon the virginals—that is, for a queene.'

If you ever get a chance to play a harpsichord you will find that you cannot change the volume much or play long notes however hard you try.

Composers therefore often added decorative 'twiddles' to their music to give the effect of accents or longer notes. Some later models have two keyboards and foot pedals that enable the player to suddenly change both volume and sound quality.

Modern copies of harpsichords and clavichords are frequently used, especially in performances of old music. A few composers even write for them today.

(a) Listen to a recording demonstrating the above Renaissance keyboard instruments.

Here are two other very popular Elizabethan instruments:

The lute

The lute, plucked like a guitar, was used both for solos and for accompanying the player's own singing of songs called AYRES. Its special music is called TABLATURE. Lutes were often available in barber's shops for the customer's entertainment. The most famous singing lutenist was the Englishman, John Dowland. He was regarded rather like one of today's pop stars.

The viol

This bowed instrument, like many Renaissance instruments, came in different sizes. The largest size was also called the viola da gamba. A complete set was called a chest of viols— after where they were stored.

Generally, a set of any one type of instrument was called a WHOLE CONSORT. A BROKEN CONSORT consisted of mixed instruments.

(b) Compare (i) a lute ayre with a modern guitar folk song, (ii) music for viol consort with music for the violin family. Discuss how the lute/guitar and viol/violin compare in shape and playing method (see pictures above and on page 5).

(c) Listen to whole and broken consort music.

In your notebook

(ii) Write a few sentences comparing the harpsichord, lute and viol with their present-day relatives. Add illustrations if you can.

 (d) Listen to 'All Creatures Now', a madrigal by John Bennet. It is from a collection honouring Queen Elizabeth I (Oriana). Follow the words as you listen:

'All creatures now are merry-minded.
W The Shepherds' daughters playing,
X The nymphs are fa-la-laing,
Yond bugle was well winded.
At Oriana's presence each thing smileth.
The flowers themselves discover:
Birds over her do hover
Music the time beguileth.
See where she comes with flowery garlands crowned.
Y Queen of all queens renowned.
Then sang the shepherds and nymphs of Diana:
Z Long live fair Oriana.'

Notice:
(i) the word and phrase-repetition;
(ii) although the same words are sung together at the beginning and elsewhere, there is 'impolite' butting in as the voices play 'copy cats' at W, X, Y and Z.
Discuss why the music suits the words at 'well winded' and 'hover'. This is called 'word painting'.

Madrigals, however, were an upper-class entertainment. Here are two 'pop' tunes from the sixteenth century. They would have been whistled, sung and played by many people. Some composers wrote VARIATIONS on the 'pop' tunes of the day. This is another 'recipe' for making music longer and more interesting. In these early variations, the notes of the tune were often divided into increasingly shorter (and quicker) ones. This is why some variations were called divisions.

Two Elizabethan 'pop' tunes:

'A Toye'

'Jhon Come Kisse Me Now'

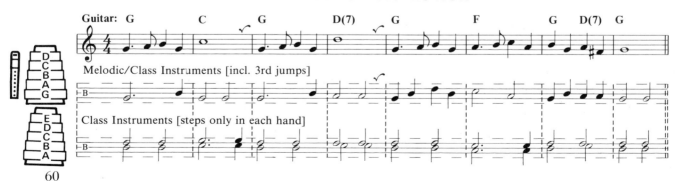

60

(e) Listen to these Elizabethan popular tunes, preferably in performances on the harpsichord. Follow the music, even through any variations of the tunes.

Things to do

9. First practise the given accompanying parts separately. Later, combine them as an accompaniment to the songs played on the piano.

10. The following groups of rhythmic ostinati are designed to accompany some of the Renaissance dance rhythms. First practise them on the instruments suggested:

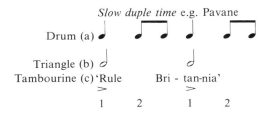

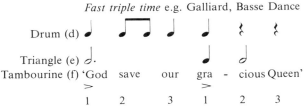

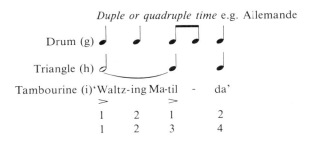

Now, as many as possible combine the rhythms of each set. Finally, just three players:
(i) Play ostinati (g), (h) and (i) as an additional accompaniment to either Elizabethan 'pop' tune, performed as above or on a recording.
(ii) Play the appropriate ostinati as an accompaniment to recordings of Renaissance dances. All work out the time of each dance first. Modify the patterns to make a good ending if necessary.

11. Turn 'A Toye' into a modern 'pop' tune. First, have a competition to see who can write the best words for it. Sing the winning entry, preferably with guitar accompaniment. Later, three pupils improvise additional swinging accompaniments using side drum and rhythm brushes, tambourine and wood block.

12. Write out the rhythm of 'A Toye' from memory.

New sounds

Regular beats, a regular time and a preference for the mixture of a 3rd have been with us for a long time now. Even today, most music—and especially the popular variety—is based on these things.

However, there are composers today who want to have a change. First listen to some of the new 'fashions' and then to do some experiments yourselves.

 (f) Listen to modern experimental music. Try to clap with the beat.

Things to do

13. In two groups and at the same tempo, count triple against quadruple time, exaggerating the loudness of each beat 1. After the start, do the first beats ever come together again?

Similarly mix the two word rhythms of Chapter 12, 10(a) and (c), repeating each as an ostinato. Finally, repeat both these activities, but with each pupil at a different tempo.

14. First revise the code on page 17 together with the advice on choice of instruments and playing instructions. Now, five pupils take turns at mixing these parts on fading instruments of the correct pitch, spacing roughly as shown:

Next, five pupils combine the above parts, but each play instead any interval of a 2nd (tone or semitone) using two beaters. Finally, the whole class, sharing instruments if necessary, perform in both the above ways, independently or under five conductors.

15. Play the following in two groups and under two conductors. We have made it clear when the sounds of both groups are meant to start or stop at the same moment. At these places, the conductors must be very alert:

When different parts are meant to start or step together, it is helpful to use some kind of GRID.

The numbers are not to be regularly counted like normal beats. They just give the approximate placing of each 'event'. The conductor must either call out each number or make a conducting gesture at each one. Sounds that start or stop at these points must coincide exactly. Between them, it is up to each player to judge when to start or stop a sound. Be careful that a conducting gesture does not make you play when you should not.

Here are two additions to the code:

wwwww⌐ A fast tremolo getting slower
vvvvvv A slow tremolo getting faster

Things to do

16. In two groups, play the two previous grids under one conductor. Use contrasted long note or fading-note instruments. For example, pitched/unpitched, 'white' notes/ 'black' notes.

17. Now play these parts in three groups. Use instruments as suggested below, damping when necessary:

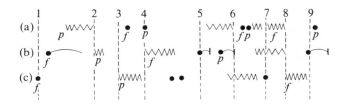

(a) Hit wood: pitched or Any 2nd (tone)

(b) Hit metal: unpitched or Any 2nd (semitone)

(c) Hit wood: unpitched or Any 3rd

18. Choose an instrument and write a part for it on a grid identical to the above. All play your parts together. Take turns at being conductor.

19. Using the same blank grid, write the code symbols as a similar part is played to you by a conductor counting the grid numbers.

20. Compose your own two- or four-part grid. Show the instruments required and get into groups to practise your pieces. Perform to the class.

21. In five groups perform the following under a conductor. Play the pitches indicated:

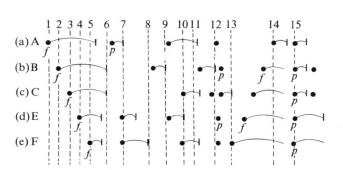

16 SIGNS OF THE TIMES

Dotted beats

Things to do

1. Combine these opening rhythms as ostinati, (a) 'Somewhere, over the rainbow' and (b) 'I've got a lovely bunch of coconuts'. Now try to write each rhythm down. After reading the following, repeat the combined ostinati looking at the given music. Change to alternating rhythms.

Rhythm (a) is straightforward. After two-beat notes (minims), one of the beats splits up into halves (quavers).

In rhythm (b), one beat splits up into thirds, others split up unequally, ending in a three-beat note. With the doubling/halving code, thirds of a beat should be impossible.

The answer is to make each beat a dotted note. There are three quavers in each ♩. Notice how a beat's worth still 'hold hands':

An Elizabethan song: 'Greensleeves'

When the beats are ♩. (as in the following song) they can still be counted in the usual way, or you may use words to get the rhythm right:

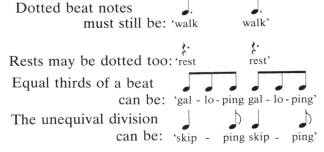

Dotted beat notes
must still be: 'walk   walk'

Rests may be dotted too: 'rest   rest'

Equal thirds of a beat
can be: 'gal - lo - ping gal - lo - ping'

The unequival division
can be: 'skip - ping skip - ping'

(a) Now follow the music as the song below is heard in a recording with lute accompaniment.
(b) Listen to duple-time pieces played on the piano or in recordings. Try to fit both 'running' and 'galloping' with the beats of each to identify those pieces having dotted beats.

Things to do

2. Practise and add the three-line stave part to the song.

3. First all repeat 'galloping' and then 'skipping' at the same tempo. Then, in three groups, combine 'walk', 'galloping' and 'skipping'. Finally, clap instead of saying the words. Always accent the first note of each group, just as you accent the first syllable of 'galloping' and 'skipping' when you say them.

4. Combine rhythms as above, but with each group changing rhythm at a signal, as follows:

5. First, all say 'walk' at the same tempo. Then, in two groups, and at the same beat tempo, say 'running' and 'galloping'. At a signal, change words. Do any syllables fit exactly against each other?

6. At the same tempo, clap as an ostinato:
(a) The opening rhythm of 'Jingle bells'.

(b) The same in its ♩. beat variation:

Now clap (a) and (b) with the appropriate version played on the piano. Next, sing the song (i) normally with ♩ beats, (ii) in its ♩. beat variation and (iii) in both versions simultaneously, in two groups.

Finally, hear/sing 'A Toye' and 'Good King Wenceslas' in their dotted beat versions.

7. Practise the following duple-time phrases, saying the rhythm words:

Later, using contrasted unpitched instruments, combine and then play in succession as a canon from X or Y. Finally, repeat each rhythm as an accompaniment to 'A Toye' (proper version).

8. Similarly treat the following, this time accompanying 'Greensleeves':

9. Repeat Chapter 12, 7, but matching the same phrases to the following ♩. beat rhythms:

Bars, bar lines, time signatures

Do you remember how, in Chapter 15, a grid helped you fit the parts together more easily? Some kind of grid would also make the normal rhythm (code) easier to read and fit together.

Let us put a line to the left of every first beat in rhythms 7(a) and (b):

Helpful guide lines like these, originally called bars and first introduced in the sixteenth century, are now called BAR LINES. Unlike the grid lines you used in Chapter 15, nothing happens on them neither do they stop the music!

The music between each bar line is called a BAR or MEASURE. Here is a triple-time rhythm of four bars with a DOUBLE BAR (LINE) to mark the end:

There is no need to print accents now as their place is clear at the beginning of each bar. There will also be no need to write the beat numbers in if the composer 'signs' the time at the beginning of each piece.

This TIME SIGNATURE consists of two numbers written above each other:

The number of beats in the bar—or the time—is given by the upper figure: e.g. **2**

The lower figure tells us which note value is to be used as the beat. For the present, we shall write the note value instead: e.g. ♩or ♩.

In your notebook

(i) In your own words, explain: bar lines, bars and time signatures.

Things to do

10. Write out the last rhythm as 'sausages on sticks'. It has been started for you:

Use a scale of ♩ = 1 inch. The 'sausages' could be cut from sticky paper, with a different colour for each value.

11. Listen to pieces played on the piano or in a recording. First identify the time of each, then the number of bars played by counting the beats quietly.

12. Repeat Chapter 13, 7. Now echo these two-bar rhythms clapped to you. Each echo and the next rhythm are to follow continuously:

13. Clap the following (i) saying the rhythm words and (ii) counting the time:

   Now, in two groups, and at the same tempo, combine (a) and (c); (a) and (b) and (b) and (c). What does this remind you about the different times?

14. Clap the following. At first, only say the rhythm words. When you count, why cannot you say 'and' for the quavers?

15. Turn to Chapter 11, 10. (a) and (b) are in triple time, (c) and (d) quadruple. Repeat the activity with these while their respective times are counted.

   Now write these four rhythms (no solfa) adding the correct time signatures and bar lines. They all begin on beat 1. Similarly, rewrite the duple-time rhythms of 8 above.

16. Take turns at playing any rhythm from 13 and 14 on a class pitched

instrument. In each case use a row of stepping letters up or down from A, C, D, or G. Change to the next note each bar.

17. Make up a word from these letters: G A B D E. Improvise an ostinato pattern using the letters of your word in any way you like. Fit against a duple-time count. Combine in various ways as previously.

18. Clap and say each rhythm before playing the following tunes:

Now sing each tune after laying the solfa 'trail'. Later, combine the tunes barred together, playing and/or singing.

19. Draw a three line stave as follows:

Now write down phrases played slowly to you in the rhythm shown. You will be told the starting-note letter, and the only jump will be an interval of a 3rd.

20. Repeat 19, but this time the rhythm will be different. Only ♩, ♩ and ♫ will be used.

21. The words of these songs fit against each other as shown. First, combine them as spoken ostinati. It will show you how well duple and quadruple mix:

                              Y   X

(a) ⅔ 'Jingle   bells, | jingle bells, | jingle all the | way' ‖

(b) 4 'Rudolf, the red-nosed reindeer | had a very shiny nose' ‖

(c) 4 'I'm   dreaming of a | white   Christmas' ‖

In three groups, perform as a rhythmic word-speaking round, at first coming in with a one-line delay. Later, come in at X and Y. Just for fun (i) speak softly until the final very loud 'Christmas' and (ii) all say the three lines in succession in your head together. Try not to change the tempo and say 'Christmas' aloud when you get to the end.

22. Take turns accompanying previous quadruple-time songs, playing the above three rhythms as ostinati. Use contrasted unpitched instruments. Later add further players using the rhythms of 7.

23. The following are either in ⅔ or ⅗ time. Work out which by fitting either 'running' or 'galloping' against them.

(a) 'My Old Man's a Dustman'   (c) 'For He's a Jolly Good Fellow'.

(b) 'Waltzing Matilda'   (d) 'What Shall We Do with the Drunken
                              Sailor?'

17 STAFF MEETING

Treble and bass staves

Things to do

1. After you have worked out how many different letters can fit on a three-line stave, see how many stave lines would be needed for all the 'white' notes on your piano.

About twenty lines would be needed for the whole piano keyboard. You can see our three-line stave buried near the middle.

But a stave of this size would be ridiculous. It would not only strain your eyes, it would prevent your reading notes quickly. Without looking at the keyboard diagram, just see how long it takes you to work out the letter name of note X down from the given B!

Fortunately, the very high and very low notes are seldom played. All we usually need are the eleven lines covering the middle of the piano. However, even this number would make life difficult when trying to count lines and spaces quickly across large intervals.

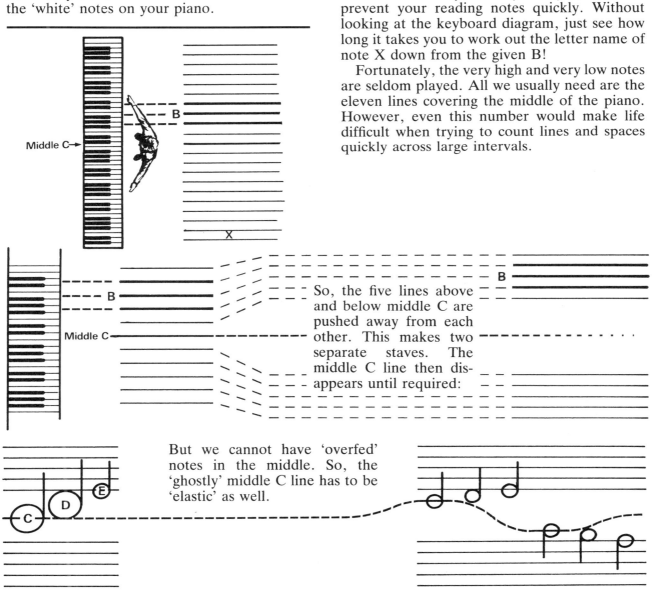

So, the five lines above and below middle C are pushed away from each other. This makes two separate staves. The middle C line then disappears until required:

But we cannot have 'overfed' notes in the middle. So, the 'ghostly' middle C line has to be 'elastic' as well.

With instruments like the piano where the right hand plays high notes amd the left hand low ones, both staves are needed. Most instruments, however, have fewer notes and are either high or low. These therefore need only the upper or lower stave.

A TREBLE CLEF is put at the beginning of each upper or TREBLE STAVE (STAFF) for the high-note (treble) instruments and high voices:

A BASS CLEF is put at the beginning of each lower or BASS STAVE (STAFF) for the low-note (bass) instruments and low voices:

The lowest instrument or voice used is also called the bass part. As most of your instruments (and your voices) are high ones, only the treble stave will be used at present.

You will now need a manuscript book or separate sheets of staved (music) paper. The treble clef is drawn like this:

Things to do

2. Looking at the above diagrams, discuss (a) why we have a five-line stave and not more or fewer lines, (b) why the middle C line is both a 'ghost' and 'elastic', (c) why the treble clef looks like a complicated G and (d) what 'clef' means in French.

3. Look at the twenty-one line stave on page 67. How many notes can fit on it? With E in the bottom space, how many other Es is there room for?

How does this compare with your piano? Now hear first, all the 'white' notes in succession upwards, and then all the Es. In both cases, follow with a finger on the piano illustrated.

If the doh symbol is placed on the bottom space, can you now say immediately how many dohs fit on this big stave?

4. The following groups of notes all spell words. If you play an instrument you should be able to work them out immediately. Others can count up or down from 'landmarks' like B on the middle line.

5. Take turns at playing the above words on the piano. Remember, on this instrument, you must play both the correct letter and at the correct octave above middle C.

6. All repeat 5, using any suitable class instrument. Play each note when directed and listen for any 'odd men out'. Try to go up and down correctly, but if your instrument is small you may have to change direction to another octave.

7. Draw a treble clef on stave paper and place notes to 'spell' ADD, BAG, DEAD, FADED, CAGED. Next, see how many different ways you can 'spell' FACE.

8. A musical spy wrote this message in code. What is it?

Now make up similar messages for others to solve.

9. Listen to three-letter words played on the piano. The smallest interval will be used each time. Identify the words (a) when given the starting letter, (b) when given the final letter and (c) without any information.

10. Looking at the treble stave, what is the interval from (a) middle C to the A above, (b) middle C to the top line, (c) the top line down to the bottom space and (d) the bottom line to the top space?

11. Work out both the letter and solfa names of the highest and lowest note(s) of all the songs in this book with a given ■

12. Follow the music of any previous song as it is played on the piano. Name the letter when the playing stops anywhere in the middle.

13. Repeat the first part of Chapter 11, 6, starting from middle C. Now write down both parts on stave paper, continuing the following, using minims but no bar lines:

Perform again. What interval mixture did you sing?

14. On separate staves, write out tunes (a) and (b) from Chapter 11, 10 again. This time, place ■ on middle C, add bar lines and the correct time signature. Sing the phrases separately and in combination as before. Accompany the sing-

ing with some pupils playing on suitable instruments. Is all this easier now that you are using an 'up and down' code?

15. Sing the following hymn as a canon in two to four parts. X indicates each delay. Finally, accompany the singing with an ostinato, repeating one or both of the bracketed phrases on any instruments.

A hymn tune: **Thomas Tallis**

Interval of a 5th

So far in your music reading you have only had to recognise

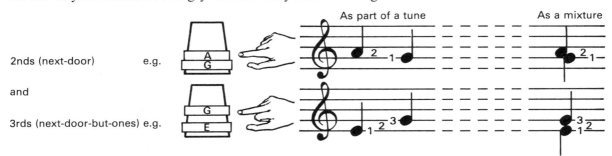

2nds (next-door)   e.g.

and

3rds (next-door-but-ones) e.g.

Now it is the turn of a larger interval:

5ths   e.g.

Just as a 3rd always measures 'line–line' or 'space–space', so a 5th measures 'line–line–line' or 'space–space–space'.

You may already know which letter belongs to each line and space. However, it is much better to read music by going up and down intervals than by working out the letter name of every note.

Of course, you must always know the name of your starting note!

Things to do

16. Use two beaters and compare the effect of 3rd and 5th mixtures in the following:

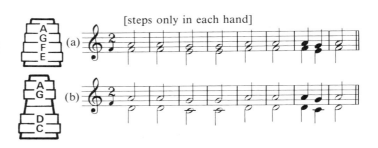

Now sing 'What shall we do with the drunken sailor'. Accompany with (a) and then with (b). Finally, add both parts simultaneously.

17. Each take a 'keyboard' instrument or draw a large keyboard of two octaves. Put your finger on a given starting letter near the middle of your instrument or drawing. You will be told to move your finger up or down a 2nd, 3rd or 5th. All those at real instruments now play where they have got to. Spot 'odd men out' and those fingering the wrong note. Score + and − points. Repeat, following a series of these moves before stopping. Finally, try both of the above while the same intervals are played instead of spoken.

18. Identify the following 2nds, 3rd and 5ths, later treating as a code as in Chapter 12, 15:

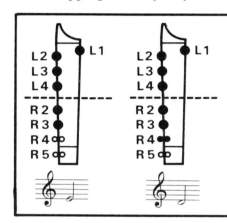

You have to use your right hand for the next two notes. Practise changing from G to E, G to D and then E to D. Now write all the notes you can play as minims, ascending on a treble stave. Practise playing up and down them.

Things to do

19. In these tunes there are intervals of a 3rd and 5th to jump across. How many jumps of each kind are there altogether? Before playing or singing as indicated, clap and count the rhythms. Combine parts barred together:

20. Compose your own tunes with these notes:

Write on the treble stave with time signature and bar lines. Begin and end on E or G, using rhythm (a) or (b):

22. A tune using the above notes will be played in the following rhythm. Write it down on the treble stave. You will be told the first note:

Select three in the same time to be written on the board. Play separately and then combine, or perform in succession as a canon with a one- or two-bar delay. Later, place doh on middle C and sing instead.

21. Treat as a code as in Chapter 12, 15:

23. Practise the playing/singing parts in the song below. Later, add (a) an ostinato based on 'Rudolf the Red-nosed reindeer'.

```
      R     R     R           R
        L     L        L
```

First tap the two hands as indicated. Then hit a wood block on every R and tap silently on every L. Play just in the chorus or throughout.
(b) A tambourine using

A song from Jamaica: 'Water come a me eye'

18   EARLY BAROQUE

The first operas

Round about the year 1600, a continued interest in ancient Greece led some Italians to try to revive Greek drama. Although little was known about it (and they certainly had no recordings!), they were sure that Greek plays had contained a lot of music and singing. So, they set about writing their own musical plays called OPERAS. The older, complicated musical fashions like the madrigal would not do for them. The story and dialogue would not be clear if everybody sang different words at the same time!

So, one character usually sang at a time, and much of the music was made very simple. This new dialogue music, called RECITATIVE, often matched the rhythm of the words and kept to just a few notes. It was accompanied by two players on a keyboard and bass instrument.

Since these played continuously throughout the work this accompaniment was called the CONTINUO. The very first operas were nearly all recitative, and must have been very boring. However, composers like Monteverdi (Italy) soon realised that operas had to have interesting music as well as tell a story clearly.

They mixed recitative with real tunes, called ARIAS. In these the singers could show off their voices—even though this usually meant that the story stopped while they were doing it!

If it made good sense, they allowed two characters to sing together in a DUET, or even more in a larger ENSEMBLE. Sometimes they included crowd scenes, so that a complete CHOIR could sing a CHORUS.

The opera usually began with an OVERTURE. This was written for whatever players were available. These would also join the continuo in other places to give variety.

The stories of these first operas came from Greek or Roman mythology, the tale of 'Orpheus in the Underworld' being the most popular. Composers also started setting Bible stories

James I   Charles I   Charles II

A.V. of   THE
Bible   COMMONWEALTH
                 Oliver Cromwell
                 CIVIL WAR
Galileo   PLAGUE
Guy Fawkes   GREAT FIRE
PILGRIM   Pepys
FATHERS   Bunyan
Bacon   Milton
    Rembrandt   Wren
Rubens   PURCELL   Defoe

to music in a similar way, but without the acting. These are called ORATORIOS. The new musical fashions also affected other types of music. However, without the aid of radio, the changes took many years to spread from Italy to the rest of Europe.

Purcell

Later in the seventeenth century, one of Britain's greatest composers, Henry Purcell, also wrote operas. Among his other music are FANTASIAS (fantasies or fancies) for viols. He be-

came organist at Westminster Abbey when only twenty. The organ, previously damaged by Cromwell's soldiers, had only just been repaired. Later, Purcell took a similar job at the Chapel Royal. His many anthems are still frequently sung today. He died, aged only thirty-six, in 1695.

The Baroque

But the seventh century really belonged to Italy. Apart from having most of the composers, Italy was the home of Stradivarius and other famous makers of the increasingly popular violin family. This family was soon to become the foundation of the orchestra.

Composers, for the first time, started writing music to suit particular instruments. For example, violins often had quick jumpy tunes or repeated notes to match the player's bowing movements. They also now wrote instructions on how their music was to be performed. Thus Italian became the language of music.

Up to now, Britain had shared the musical 'First Division' with Italy and some other countries. From the seventeenth century, apart from Purcell, British composers found themselves relegated to the 'Fourth Division'. Until very recently, British musicians sometimes changed to a foreign version of their name—just to sound impressive.

Some people disliked the new musical fashions, particularly the jerky recitative, its exaggerated expression and the antics of 'show-off' singers. These would often hold up the performance, adding decorative scales and 'twiddles' to their arias. The unnatural male sopranos, often treated like today's pop stars,

73

were the worst offenders. Sometimes just their first note was applauded for several minutes. The worst features of the new style, which also affected the other arts, were likened to a distorted pearl called a barocco. From this we get the BAROQUE period.

In your notebook

(i) (Copy, completing the words)
An o——is a play in which all the words are sung. The simple music in speech rhythm that tells the story is called r——.

O——usually begin with an o——and also contain solo a—— and c——for a choir. Bible stories in the same style, but not acted, are called o——.

(a) Listen to (i) early operatic recitative, (ii) a 'show-off' aria and (iii) church music by Purcell.

Assignment

(A) Apply Assignments (C) and (D) (page 32) or A (page 56) to this period.

19   BOY MEETS GIRL

Recitative and imitation

Nearly all operas are love stories. Most early ones were written by Italian and, later, French composers. However, Purcell's 'Dido and Aeneas', first performed in 1689, was written for a London girls' school.

The opera is based on the Roman story about the love of the Queen of Carthage (Dido) for a Trojan prince (Aeneas), and how the witches deceive him into forsaking her.

Certain earlier musical fashions returned in the seventeenth century. For example, both 'word painting' and 'copy cat' musical conversation called IMITATION occur in this opera (see Extracts A and B).

Extracts from 'Dido and Aeneas'   **Purcell**

(a) Listen to parts of the above opera, trying to catch all the words.

(i) The overture: written for the new violin family, which had now become as popular as the more gentle viols. Both the slow first part and the faster second part seem to suggest that the story is sad. Although the music of the first part could have been sung or played on almost anything, the jumpy second part is only possible on a bowed instrument.

(ii) The first solo: sung by Dido's lady-in-waiting, Belinda. The style is a mixture of recitative and aria. Identify the continuo accompaniment. Notice word painting on the words 'shake' and 'flowing'. A chorus follows.

(iii) The cave scene: hear real recitative on just a few notes as the sorceress conjures up her witches. Next comes a witches' chorus. The sorceress then forecasts Dido's doom followed by a chorus of witches delighting in their mischief. Notice how the voices enter in imitation (Extract A) sharing a jolly good laugh. This is shortly repeated.

Later, in a duet, two witches conjure up a storm (Extract B). Notice imitation and showy 'word painting' on the word 'storm'. The witches then sing a chorus as they prepare a charm in their cave. It must be big as it has an echo!

(iv) The closing scene set on the quayside:

A sailor's song is repeated by a chorus of sailors. Notice imitation at the beginning of the chorus. Although there appear to be ladies in this navy, sailors obviously have not changed much. Just listen to the words!

Things to do

1. Make up your own recitative. Use this conversation, which we also hope is mythical!
(*Teacher*) 'This is the last time I'm going to tell you not to be cheeky.'
(*Class*) 'That's what you said last time.'
(*T*) 'But this time I mean it.'
(*C*) 'We shall see.'
(*T*) 'Don't be cheeky.'
(*C*) 'You see what we mean!'

First chant each class part together until you agree about the speech rhythms. Then sing the conversation in the same rhythms, using note G for the teacher and E for the class. A piano 'continuo' can be added.

2. Clap the opening rhythm of Purcell's 'Sailor's Song' as an ostinato. Accompany the recording.

'Come a-way fel-low sai-lors'

3. Echo back short tunes (like the witches).
4. Practise this 'witch chorus', singing (a) me, soh, lah and (b) 'ha ha ha' in a fiendish way:

Now, in two groups, repeat the phrase four times, the second coming in at X or Y.

Ground bass

Imitation, echoes and rounds are very similar musical 'recipes'. Purcell was also particularly fond of repeating a low-pitched melodic ostinato called a GROUND (BASS). 'Above the ground', the singer or other instruments go their own way. There is a very beautiful example of this at the end of the opera. Deserted by Aeneas, Dido stabs herself, but still manages to sing a lament before dying—operas are not always very sensible!

(b) First follow Extract C with your finger as it is played several times on the piano. The notes descend in semitones, as if the bass itself is dying—or being slowly lowered into a grave. During the solo, follow the bass in the same way. How many times is it repeated? Finally, discuss which famous people could have attended the opera's first performance in 1689.

Things to do

5. In groups, (a) some pupils slowly repeat CAGE as descending ♩. , eight times on a large glockenspiel, metallophone or other bass intrument, (b) the remainder improvise on the same four notes (in any order) using treble instruments.

6. Again compare the effect of 3rd and 5th mixtures as you play the following. Later, combine the parts:

75

7. You are now ready to play and then combine these 'zig-zag' phrases using the above notes. First practise the movements in playing

to the rhythms of 'walk' and 'galloping'. Compare the notation with that on page 57. Which rule is broken here?

Finally, using suitable contrasted intruments, combine all the parts of 6 and 7.

8. First practise the following:

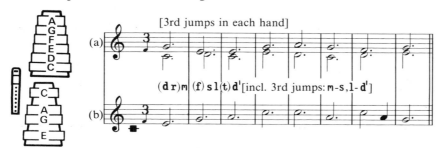

Now combine them, playing/singing as indicated. Finally, repeat the phrases above a descending scale from C to C, played four times as a ground bass, one note to a bar.

9. Repeat 8, but this time vary the upper parts as in a real ground bass.
(i) Improvise four different repeated note or 'zig-zag' versions of (a);
(ii) similarly change the rhythm of (b).

10. Improvise triple time parts above A CAGED BEE bass played four times in the rhythm:

Choose any indicated notes in each bar.

11. Similarly treat AGED BAD EGG:

This time, choose two or more notes from the words to play throughout, in any rhythm.

12. Finally, write one or more phrases on a treble stave to fit 10. Choose notes as before (and at 8ves you can play!). The only jumps may be 3rds and 5ths. Use the above rhythm or your own. Join four phrases into one long tune and combine tunes above the repeated bass. Repeat with 11.

20 TIME FOR A REST

The minim and semibreve rests

Things to do

1. Learn or sing a verse of the hymn 'Onward Christian Soldiers'. Now, in two groups, clap its rhythm against a regular beat. For how long does the last note of each phrase last?

Each final note: ○ lasts for four crotchet beats and is called a SEMIBREVE.

Here are two, showing how semibreves continue the halving and doubling rhythm code:

Although the ○ looks like a nought, it is certainly not four beats'-worth of nothing. It must continue sounding through four beats and then not stop immediately:

Neither are long rests 'nothings' or 'holidays'. This is the SEMIBREVE REST:

It must also have four beats pumping through it.

The same symbol is also used as a rest for any complete bar:

even though there is not really enough room for it in times like 3 and 2 .

Here is a MINIM REST: Like the minim note, it has two crotchet beats pumping through it: Remember:

Semibreve	wHole bar	Semibreve
Ship	Heavy	Suspended from
Sinks	Hangs	Sky

See how 'sausages on sticks' make the different note values clear:

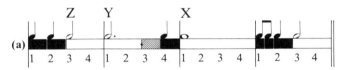

And how notes can be replaced by rests of the same duration:

In your notebook

(i) Draw and label a semibreve note and rest, showing how four crotchet beats fit against each. (ii) Similarly draw and label a minim rest.

Things to do

2. All mark time at the same tempo. At a signal, stop but still 'imagine' the movements. Restart marking time after a given number of 'steps'.
3. In four groups, combine the different note values set out on this page. Either all clap or use contrasted instruments. At a signal, change to the value below—or return to the first one.
4. In three groups, similarly combine ○, ♩ and ♩ . Repeat, but with each group alternating its note value with the matching rest.
5. In two or more groups, clap (a) and (b)

77

above in succession as a canon from X, Y, or Z. 'Nod' the beats through the longer notes and rests.

6. Similarly treat these rhythms:

7. Combine these (whispered) word ostinati:

8. In groups of four, make up and perform similar rhythmic patterns. Experiment with animal noises or sounds like 'whee', 'zoom' and 'doink' for different effects.

9. First practise these parts separately. Say the given words loudly in the correct rhythm, and each 'rest' beat in your head:

Now, say the words in three groups, solving the mystery sentence.

10. Why is this 'mystery' harder to solve than 9?

11. Compose your own mystery sentence. Break it up between two or more parts as above, changing the spelling of some syllables.
12. Play (a) or sing to solfa. Then perform (b), imagining the notes now replaced by rests:

Ornaments

As long notes are not holidays and should be filled with sound, they are sometimes 'fattened up' a little. Instruments that can keep going until the player gets tired are no problem. Short-sound instruments (and the others, of course) can have a tremolo, SHAKE, TRILL or ROLL on one or more notes to keep the sound alive during long notes.

Although some instruments have their own special signs for these things, we shall only use ∿ . Shakes and other ORNAMENTS were often used in the Baroque period.

Things to do

13. Each take a class pitched or unpitched instrument. Now practise playing ∿ , ∿ and ∿ together, using the method and number of beaters suitable for each instrument. Count as you play, remembering that a two-beat note lasts until the third beat, and so on. Damp if necessary.
14. Repeat 4, 5 and 6, using contrasted instrument and adding a ∿ to all notes longer than a crotchet.
15. Use unpitched short-sound or fading-sound instruments and perform as in 6:

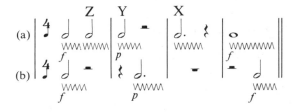

78

16. Practise these parts, and later combine:

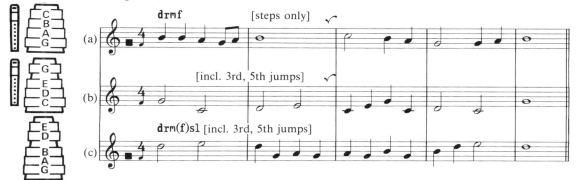

Listen to Purcell's Five-Part Viol Fantasia. One viol plays middle C throughout. Accompany it playing 47 semibreves on any instruments.

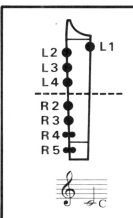

Here is the lowest note that the recorder can produce—middle C. Think about why the 'middle' can also be the 'lowest'.

Only apply the gentlest air pressure for the low notes or they will squeak. Practise going from middle C to each of the other notes that you know in turn.

You are now ready to play the parts indicated above.

Experiments with rests

Silences are important in all kinds of music, even though not all players need be resting at the same time. If silences, sounds or beats do not have to be measured exactly, you can often do without a conductor.

Remember, unless told otherwise, in this sort of music notes of any or no pitch may mix together.

Things to do

17. Take any class instrument, and privately decide the tempo at which you are going to count 1 to 40 in your head. Decide also on which numbers you are going to play four single short sounds, mixing them loud and soft. All start counting at a signal.

18. Choose one of the song openings from Chapter 16, 21. Decide also your own tempo, how many beats you are going to count before saying the words rhythmically, how many times you are going to say them and the number of beats between each repetition. Again, all start from a signal. Vary it by (a) all whispering and (b) including both loud and soft repetitions.

19. Instead of a conductor's grid, you can use something like the bosun's code on page 17. The sounds are fitted to the counting of seconds.

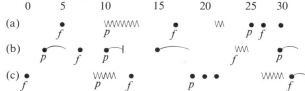

Using appropriate instruments, combine the above (i) while real seconds are counted, (ii) each counting 'seconds' silently, not necessarily starting together.

20. Get into groups and compose and perform your own two- or three-part piece as above.

21. Return to previous songs. You will now be able to play all the parts marked Class Instruments. The parts marked Melodic Instruments can be played on the descant recorder. All music (incl. songs) with given ■ may also be sung to solfa.

Index